ENGLISH OUT THERE

English Out There - Intermediate TD4

A modern English course incorporating social interaction in the real world and online

60 hours of lesson plans and student worksheets

Copyright © 2009 by Languages Out There Ltd

All characters and images contained in this book are copyrighted creations of Languages Out There Ltd and their licensors

All rights Reserved. The worksheets pages in this book may be copied for classroom use. This use is restricted to one book only per study group or class of students, not exceeding twenty individuals. Other books must be purchased for other study groups or classes of students. The use of one book to copy across an institution or on different sites of an institution is prohibited.

The purchase of this book gives you a 50% discount when you pay for a membership subscription to our website www.languagesoutthere.com which gives you access to lots more Out There teaching and learning materials, articles and information for teachers. To claim your subscription just email info@languagesoutthere.com and you will receive a reply requesting some information from the book. Simply reply with the required information and you will receive an email with a promotional code to enter into the website to claim your discount.

No part of this publication may be reproduced or transmitted in any form or by any means, electronic or mechanical, including photocopy (other than specified above), recording, or any information and retrieval system, without permission in writing from the copyright holder/publisher, except in the case of brief quotations embodied in critical articles reviews.

Cover, cover art and interior design by:

Sinead Madden and Guardian Professional

Library of Congress Control Number: 0000000000

ISBN: 978-0-9561589-0-1

Printed in the United States of America via Lulu press (www.lulu.com)

Publisher: Languages Out There Ltd, 10 Coptic Street, London, WC1A 1NH, www.languagesoutthere.com

This first Out There Intermediate course book is dedicated to every friendly student, teacher, agent and school that has helped and supported us over the years and most of all to my mother, without whose generosity and support none of this would ever have been possible.

We got there in the end.

Intermediate English Out There – Contents

				Page
Introduction				1
Instructions for Out There teachers				4
Level 4	Topic	Aim	Language Focus	
Lesson 1	My city	To get recommendations for activities in a city	Recommending, suggesting and vocabulary for activities	18
Lesson 2	Observation - people and events	To describe people and what they were doing	Past continuous, past simple and appearance, adjectives of description	24
Lesson 3	Manners	To discuss differences in manners between individuals and nationalities	Idioms and phrases used to give opinions	30
Lesson 4	Technology and possibilities	To enable students to discuss future possibilities	Modals of probability, possibility and certainty	34
Lesson 5	Shopping	To find and describe items	Shopping vocabulary, comparatives/ superlatives	40
Lesson 6	The past of a town or city	To talk about the past	Past simple passive	44
Lesson 7	Magazines and newspapers	To discuss magazines and reading	Present perfect and vocabulary on magazines and reading	50
Lesson 8	Diaries/slang/true stories	To enable students to talk and write about past events	Past continuous/past simple	56
Lesson 9	Travel advice	To get travel and tourist advice	Expressing degrees of obligation and advice - modals	62
Lesson 10	Beauty	To assess whether ideas of beauty are cross-cultural	Adjectives	68
Lesson 11	Lies	To enable students to make admissions and apologise	Should have + past participle, I wish I had + past participle. Formal/informal	74
Lesson 12	Jobs	To enable students to find out information about jobs	Vocabulary on jobs and skills	80
Lesson 13	The weather - how does it affect you?	To enable students to talk about the weather and how it makes them feel	Weather vocabulary, expressing emotions, feelings	86
Lesson 14	Fears	To talk about fears and phobias, using past tenses	Past perfect vs past simple	90
Lesson 15	Music	To review and talk about music	Adjectives to describe music	96
Lesson 16	Food	To enable students to discuss food and find out people's favourite dishes	Vocabulary on food preparation and phrases	102
Lesson 17	Lottery	To talk about what you would do if you were a millionaire	Second conditional	108
Lesson 18	Queues	To discuss the issue of queuing, helpful or annoying	Vocabulary on cultural differences	114
Lesson 19	Health problems, treatments and advice	To enable students to discuss health and find treatments	Vocabulary related to common health problems, remedies and advice	120
Lesson 20	Sleep and dreams	To enable students to find out about dreams and sleep	Connectors and vocabulary related to dreams	126

Introduction

This book is the first in a series of six that combine all of our tried and tested English Out There lesson plans for teachers with photocopiable student worksheets.

There are twenty three-hour lesson plans in this book with photocopiable student worksheets.

What we say here will only take a few minutes to read and then the rest will be up to you, so please, relax, open your mind a little and read on.

Summary for Teachers, our teacher delivered lesson plans:

- Are specially designed to be used in the real world (English speaking countries) and online (non-English speaking countries) using Skype, language teaching websites and online language exchange websites for real practice of the target language

- Have been taught hundreds of times by many teachers and really work incredibly well

- Have been re-written and edited by experienced writers and editors after six years of teaching and testing development

- Will save you hours of lesson planning time and are ready to teach as soon as you photocopy or download them

- Will inspire your students, boost their confidence and maintain their motivation levels as they prove to themselves Out There that they can 'do it'

- Enable you to actually teach and not worry about planning, timings, materials and fillers

My name is Jason West. I have been involved in owning and running English language schools in London for almost twenty years. My second successful language teaching company, Languages Out There, has been operating for over seven years. Since July 2001 it has developed a way of teaching and learning English that is very natural, brain-friendly, challenging and fun. We have taught our lessons to thousands of paying students from all over the world and every single one has completed a leaving questionnaire. Since we started, 94% have said that they would recommend us to their friends.

Before I explain what we do, why we do it and how we do it I just want to tell you how much time and effort has gone into the creation of these unique teaching and learning materials. Our lesson plans are based upon a design and format that we experimented with in the summer of 2001. My colleagues and I tried numerous lesson plans on real students in central London and after about four months of testing and discussion we settled on a format and timings for our lessons that gave us the optimal input time that allowed our students to work with and absorb new language to the point where they were then confident and able to use it in the real world with people they had not met before…the Out There section of the lesson plan.

The idea of the programme was to create a series of lesson plans around the twenty most important areas of language that come up in conventional course books and to be able to speak and understand that language at each level. As we created the lesson plans we taught them and then adjusted them to improve their effectiveness. We continued doing that for six full years of teaching to students from around the world who came to London to improve their English skills.

So, every one of our lesson plans has been taught hundreds of times. It has been amended on the basis of the feedback from many different teachers who have taught it and it has improved every single time. In 2006 we asked Tim Bowen, a very well-known teacher trainer and English language teaching author to help us edit our lesson plans for publication. At that time the lesson plans contained exercises and content that we had created ourselves. We re-wrote some of the exercises, adapted some content and created our new graphics and a new 'look and feel'. In 2007, with Tim's help, we employed some very experienced English language teaching materials writers to again re-write some of the lesson plans and incorporated some content from the Guardian who worked with us at that time. Then Tim, my colleague Jon Jones and I edited them intensively. It nearly drove us mad as there was a lot to do!

Finally, we completed all two hundred and forty lesson plans, both those for teachers and those for students to study themselves. There are over two thousand five hundred pages of lesson plans and attached student worksheets in total.

One of the things that make our teaching and learning lesson plans unique is the time it has taken to publish them and the amount of real teaching and testing of the materials that has been involved in their creation. I can honestly say that the lesson plans work extremely well and that students appreciate their ability to help them improve their English communication skills and confidence quickly and enjoyably. Also, teachers really enjoy teaching with them as they actually let them teach by removing worries about lesson planning, finding supplementary materials and getting timings right in class.

Why we have created these lesson plans:

I ran a British Council accredited English school in central London for eight years and got tired of students arriving and telling us that they had used the course book we had just given them (actually, I was embarrassed!). I thought that there had to be a better way to study English in London. A way that was much more interactive, realistic and challenging; that took students out into the real world and made everything they did with the language much more real. I also thought they needed a better deal if they wanted a short course of one to four weeks and wanted to improve quickly, see London, meet the locals and have an amazing linguistic experience. I created English Out There to do just that.

The idea was to make learning English much more real and contextually relevant; to get students out of the classroom and out into the English speaking world every day to practise language with local people in interesting places and hope that it helped them to improve quicker.

It did.

We knew we needed to think very carefully and differently about how we taught because we were asking the teacher and the students to leave the safety of the classroom and go out into the real world. We worked out how to make every single lesson as effective as the others by using a clear structure for each and every session. This helped us to manage the learner journey and maintain the quality of each and every single student's personal learning experience. Instead of creating materials for a classroom (i.e. finite space) we looked in towards the learner's individual learning experience and sought to manage their experiences and emotions because we realised that we could not control the real world (i.e. infinite space).

Once we got our system established and as we grew in confidence ourselves we started to notice students improving very quickly. We had focused on communication and speaking and listening skills and our level placement test was (and still is) an interview with no test of reading or writing. Because of this if a student couldn't speak they went into the beginner or elementary class. When they were there they often found the language taught in the classroom to be easy but then they had to go out and use it with people they had never met before. Because the language was easy they could concentrate on controlling their anxiety and preparing to speak to people in public. To help them we paired them with more naturally confident students and the teacher also stayed close-by to provide emotional and physical support.

I remember one Japanese student from the early days; I think her name was Emi. When she arrived to start her four-week course she wouldn't speak and was very shy. So we put her in elementary. After four weeks of fifteen hours per week and just before she went home I bumped into her outside my office and remembered her from her first day at school. "How are you Emi?" I asked. "Great!" she said, "I can speak now", and then she started speaking at great speed to me, with huge confidence, in English.

I spoke about Emi to Georgina Moon, our Director of Studies and the person who had helped me to create the Out There lesson plan format. Georgina told me that no one could shut Emi up now and that she had gone from elementary to intermediate (up two levels) in just four weeks. We were a bit baffled, but excited. This was happening with other students too so I thought I should investigate properly.

I started reading some serious academic books about linguistics and language learning. I had studied some psychology at university years ago and had always found human memory fascinating and had enjoyed the lectures I attended given by a Professor Mike Gruneberg.

I found a book called 'A cognitive approach to language learning' by Professor Peter Skehan. His book was a revelation to me. It was highly academic and all about psycholinguistics, in other words, the application of psychology to the learning of languages. At the end of his book he described some ideas on how to apply what he had written about. They were very close to what we had created, almost by accident. I even wrote to Peter Skehan to tell him what we were doing and he replied and said he could see why it was working as I had described, but that no one had ever tried something like it on the kind of scale we were doing it or even outside of a laboratory. I still have his email.

So, I began to read more and more linguistics and psycholinguistics books and read Krashen, Pinker and others and have come to a number of conclusions about what we do, they are:

- **It makes enormous scientific sense**

- **It works because it is much more brain-friendly than the conventional way of teaching and learning languages**

- **It is very challenging for the learner but if you give it a go you will get big rewards in terms of fluency and confidence and it will help you to make your 'passive' language knowledge 'active' (this last description of what our lessons do was dreamt up by Serbian students training to be English teachers at Belgrade University who still come and do our course in London).**

What we have created is definitely not for everyone who wishes to improve their language skills because it involves a little bravery for the first one or two lessons and the re-designing of your own internal learning strategy. But, once you have had a go and felt the buzz of successfully speaking to a stranger using language you have just been taught or learnt you will understand that the language can easily and naturally become linked to the unique places, topics, emotions, smells, sights and sounds that occur during every Out There session.

Happenings and experiences are memorable to the human brain, our lesson plans manage them in a way that means every single learner has their own unique and special learning experience every single time and it is that that enables them to remember language they have learned and use it again in the future.

How to use our lesson plans:

Teachers in English speaking countries - teach the first part in a classroom or quiet public area (if you are not employed by a school you can schedule classes anywhere using www.meetup.com and charge students to attend, i.e. be your own boss), print off our student worksheets that come with each lesson plan and take a piece of portable whiteboard from www.magicwhiteboard.co.uk (these stick to anything and are disposable and cheap)

Teachers in non-English speaking countries - teach the first part of the lesson in one or two parts, you can include some role play and other materials to expand it if you like, and then get the students to do the Out There practice part online using Skype forums or online language exchange websites such as www.italki.com, www.mylanguageexchange.com. www.myngle.com, there are many of them and they are mostly free for language exchange with fluent and native speakers. Ask you students to record themselves speaking to people using the language from the lesson and then to send you their best audio clips for assessment and comment. Then in the next class have a feedback discussion about what happened with each of them, discuss any new vocab they heard and generally consolidate the learning experience.

Learners in taught classes - relax, chill, don't worry, just follow the class and then be brave and speak to a few people, but don't forget to clearly say "Excuse me, I'm learning English can I ask you a few questions". Those are the magic words and what they say very quickly are many important things: 1. I'm not from your country 2. I want to speak your language with you and communicate in a friendly way 3. I don't want any money 4. I don't want a signature 5. All I want is some help for a few minutes. And if you say that and they are sitting down, not doing much and not in a rush, they will be happy to speak to you and then you have an incredible opportunity to have a truly amazing human experience with someone you have never met before which will be truly memorable.

Please make sure you read the full instructions after this introduction.

So, available exclusively from our website, there are 360 hours of unique English Out There teacher delivered lesson plans over six levels from beginner to advanced and up to 360 hours of self-study English Out There lesson plans. There is also our full Out There provider manual for download which tells you how to plan your own Out There lessons and much more detailed tips and instructions on how to use the lesson plans plus interesting articles about language teaching and learning.

In 2009 we intend to start adding new lesson plans; we already have some in development. These new lesson plans will continue to be top quality, tested and taught by us and professionally produced before publication on the website.

Email us at info@languagesoutthere.com to claim your 50% discount on membership now or just tell us what you and your students think of our materials, we'd love to hear from you.

Cheers

Jason

Instructions for teachers using LOT lessons

What is a LOT lesson?

A *LOT* lesson provides a new and alternative way of practising a language, providing the learner with everything they need to start communicating in real situations from the very first lesson. It gives them the opportunity to practice with fluent or native speakers, and provide them with an insight into the culture and values of the country first–hand, rather than from a book. The cultural input is as important a feature of the lesson as the language and in each lesson the two are combined – through the topic, the venue, people and the materials. The result is a language learner who has both a linguistic and social confidence, and an appreciation of both.

What do I need to run a language course using Languages Out There materials?

All you need to run a successful lesson are the following:

- Training room or classroom or a free friendly public space such as on www.meetup.com
- Teacher(s)
- *LOT* lesson plans
- Photocopies
- Possibly a cheap reusable and light whiteboard from www.magicwhiteboard.co.uk
- Lesson file and updated log of local venues that have been used for activity sessions (stage 2 – see below)

Is any support available once my LOT lessons are up and running?

As part of your license agreement we will provide advice and support where needed. You can contact us on Skype at: jasonoutthere or email us.

How is each lesson delivered?

LOT lessons were developed from original *Out There* lessons. They were delivered by teachers on actual language courses, and student practice always took place in the real world, which limited them to use by study abroad schools.

We have adapted the lessons to enable students to also practice online using *VoIP*, a VoIP (Voice over Internet Protocol) application, which is a web-based telephone with some clever additional features, most people have heard of Skype, which is free to download and make international phone calls via the Internet. Students can be taught the first half of the lesson in class and then practice their language skills *Out There* in the real world or online with fluent or native speakers, either in school or at home in their own time.

Each lesson is three hours long, and is divided into three stages. The three stages are inextricably linked to form a complete, self-contained lesson. The first stage takes place in the classroom (approximately 75–80 minutes but it can be split). The second stage takes place at the designated venue for that lesson (approximately 45 minutes) or online using VoIP, and the third stage takes place either at a café or other suitable venue, or alternatively back in the classroom. We recommend that real world activity lessons be completed from start to finish in one three hour session.

With the added feature of *VoIP*, schools all over the world can now use the teacher lessons plans and their students can simply use the software to practise with native speakers without actually having to be in a country that uses the target language.

VoIP is also useful for schools that are in remote or non-urban environments and don't have the full range of venues that other larger locations have.

Lesson structure and aims

Each three-hour lesson is divided into three stages:

1st stage - 'Language Input' (in the classroom)

2nd stage - 'Out There Activity' – using outside venue or VoIP

3rd stage - 'Results' (a debrief at café/bar/park/any other suitable venue)

Each lesson provides the learner with new language and skills, and the format for the lesson is designed to make it clear to the learner that learning has taken place. Learners are introduced to the language content of the lesson and the aims of the lesson are made explicit. At the end of the lesson it is demonstrated that the learners have acquired competence at the language skills they have focussed on for the session through the 'results' session. The evidence of learning is shown by the learner's completion of the 'task', which simultaneously constitutes the motivating element of the lesson. It is this end task that supports the framework for the lesson.

The function and aim of each stage can be expressed as follows:

Stage	Aims	Location
Language Input	Set the task and aims of the lesson Introduce the language and vocabulary necessary to complete the task	Classroom
Out There Activity	Provide the learners with the opportunity to practise the target language with native speakers, and/or Provide the learners with exposure to the target language and/or Provide the learners with the opportunity to obtain information on a topic	Out There or using VoIP
Result	Demonstrate that learning has taken place through the completion of the task. Enable the teacher to clarify any areas of confusion arising from language or content in the second hour Provide the teacher with the opportunity to consolidate, extend and develop the target language	Classroom or café/bar etc

What are the benefits of practising Out There with LOT lessons?

The benefits of a LOT lesson are many and varied, both to the learners and the teacher.

Learners get a more direct and practical language session that involves them getting real contact with the language and culture, using their new language with native speakers. They also get a tangible feeling of communicative success at the end of every lesson resulting in a definite confidence boost. Plus they have the opportunity to explore their local environment and have a lot of fun. Often students don't realise how much they are learning and how much language is retained. Each of our lessons enables individual learners to create their own story, or mind map with the target language, task and interpersonal interaction. In the real world this becomes multi-sensory with smells, sounds and emotions becoming linked to the language. This enables learners to recall the language more easily the next time they need to use it. Research has shown that active learning, such as the language experiences through the Out There tasks, can improve effective

recall of language considerably. [Top tip: Get your students to video or record their conversations with their mobile phones and look at them later].

When practising online, students are able to record their conversations and save them for later use. This facilitates repeated listening and self-analysis. Files can be sent to their teachers as homework and can easily be transferred to iPods and MP3 players. Instructions for how to work with the lesson plans online are provided at the end of this document and you can print them and give them to your students.

Teachers and Course providers get a new and engaging course that is totally compatible with their conventional course products that they can integrate with their current course programme. You can, for example teach *LOT* lessons once or more a week as a refreshing change and, in the summer, run it as a stand alone short course.

Due to the nature of *LOT materials* every course is different and unique to the school that teaches it. You can choose the locations that you use for every *Out There* practice session your students have, either in real life or online making it personal to them and their individual learning.

LOT lessons utilises resources that have already been paid for as part of the school's normal overheads (teaching staff, copier and rooms) enabling the school to run courses at very little extra expense. You could use the entire programme as a short course in peak season and save on purchasing course books, printing and using the learning materials as often as you like within your language school. Alternatively you can run two start times in the morning in the same classroom, thus using valuable classroom space much more cost effectively; with just three classrooms you could schedule six classes in the morning. When up and running, the course is capable of providing a considerable boost to the profitability of the school and increasing its capacity at the same time.

How does LOT fit in with my current course programme?

The focus on practical language and the opportunity for real practice that *LOT* affords the learner, make the lessons the ideal compliment for more traditional courses that often stress language input over actual production. A LOT lesson is very active and a lot of fun, and compliments a book-based exam course. In this way a LOT course can either be run on its own or in conjunction with a conventional course. In peak periods it is a great stand-alone short course. Individual lessons can easily be inserted into longer and more conventional courses.

Schools can also offer students one or two weeks of *LOT lessons* at the start of a long study-abroad course and LOT is ideal for use during pre-sessional courses. Longer language courses of 24 or 36 weeks or an academic year can easily have between one and four weeks of *lessons* integrated into them. *LOT lessons are* a great way to quickly boost confidence, promote cultural awareness, improve rusty speaking and listening skills and help students get to know the local area. It could make sense to your school to start teaching LOT lessons this way. You could refer to it as a 'soft-landing' for longer course students, whilst they adjust to the local way of life.

Levels - how do we place students when the lessons are used to create a short course?

Recent addendum: There is increasing research evidence to suggest that learners are probably best placed to decide on their own level and thus choose the class they attend. This is what we would recommend for teachers using our lesson plans as part of a series of lessons scheduled on www.meetup.com.

The levels of our lesson plans all correspond to the Common European Framework of Reference for Languages

However…we have operated a bit differently up till now when it comes to placement testing. Due to the high priority that *LOT lessons* place on speaking and listening, and the focus on situational competence rather than written grammatical accuracy, learners should be placed in a class according to their competence in spoken English. Learners are therefore not given a written paper testing discrete items of grammar and vocabulary, but are tested orally by the school manager/director of studies or an experienced teacher. A short conversation with the prospective learner about themselves, their past experience and future plans should be sufficient to place them appropriately. A short task of replying to an imaginary situation can also help assess the level.

The placement test (see appendix 1) is the one used by *English Out There* in London where students exclusively take *these* lessons in the form of a short course. This can be used as a template or a flexible prototype. It includes general questions that cover a number of topics and can prompt interviewees to communicate and use a variety of structures. The questions can be altered according to the conversation as it develops with the student being assessed and written and marked in the spaces provided. The aim of this assessment conversation should be made clear to the students so they feel comfortable. It is also worth paying attention to details like posture and setting to make students them feel less like they are 'under the spotlight'!

The placement is done according to understanding and the responses given by the student. The assessment of the level should be based on the following elements:

- Ability to communicate effectively
- Fluency
- Range of vocabulary
- Successful completion of task/response to
- Accuracy
- Pronunciation

The following is a selection of linguistic points that broadly correspond to each level of the course syllabus, and will help assess the level of competency and the placement:

1. Beginner

A student that manages to greet, introduce themselves, and say what nationality they are (skills taught in Beginner's level), can be asked simple questions about their occupation, or hobbies, or family, that follow in the placement test. If the communication stops here and the questions are not understood, or if the student's answers reflect very basic communication the student can be placed in a Beginner's class, otherwise the placement test can continue with more questions/prompts.

2. Elementary

The interviewed student should be able to give information about everyday life, possess enough vocabulary to name their occupation or hobbies with ease, and show understanding of most of the questions that follow. The ability to understand and give some basic responses indicates that the student can be placed in Elementary. If the average mark of the responses to the questions is above 2 (which corresponds to Elementary) the test can continue with a situation task, preferably one of the first three. Otherwise, it is not advisable to continue.

3. Pre-Intermediate

In order for a student to be placed in this level, they should be able to respond to the previously mentioned prompts with more than one word. They should also be able to express feelings or attitudes and answer a question on directions (e.g. was it easy to find the school? How did you get here?). If the student is not able to cope with the above or with giving simple opinions, explanations, or making suggestions, Pre-Intermediate is the level of the placement.

4. Intermediate

Students at this level should be able to use language to explain or describe things like their job, hobbies or accommodation, with more than single nouns and one or two adjectives. Lack of language to discuss situations of daily life, to make or describe future plans, and to agree and disagree politely, or the use of simple sentences without relative clauses or 'should, would, could' modal verbs when necessary, also indicate that students should be in Intermediate level.

5. Upper-Intermediate

Students should be placed in this level if they are fluent and communicate easily, having performed the tasks for the previous levels, but still make some errors of accuracy, mispronounce certain sounds, make errors in stress placement or lack vocabulary when expressing emotions, wishes or hopes, or when discussing hypothetical situations.

6. Advanced

When the competency of the students is high and they have successfully responded to the questions of all the other levels but lack language for complex discussions and make minor errors of accuracy, then the suggested level is advanced.

Out There venues

There are a variety of locations for the activity, ranging from museums and galleries to stations, department stores and the street. Every lesson plan recommends the type of real life location that is best for the purpose of the lesson and Resources available to facilitate this practice, such as web sites.

Requirements of a venue

There are a number of initial considerations to bear in mind when selecting venues for the *Out There* task in the second hour. Venues should preferably be:

- Free (if possible, which may necessitate advance booking)
- Within approximately fifteen minutes from the school (either on foot or public transport)
- Welcoming to groups of visitors

Visiting the venue before the lesson

It is essential that the teacher visit a venue before a lesson is planned around it for the first time. This is not only to enable the teacher to prepares properly for the lesson but also ensure the teacher plans the route to take there, plans the timing, and ensures that there is a suitable area for the group to meet up for the third stage of the lesson (either a cafe within the building or somewhere suitable nearby). Where a teacher is following a lesson that has already been taught by a colleague in the school they should consult the updated log in a file created to store the lesson plans.

Admission requirements

When taking a class to a venue for the first time it is important that the teacher checks all of the admission requirements.

Taking groups Out There for LOT lessons

Use the 'welcome' sheet (Appendix 2) and customise it. It contains important rules for the students for when they are taking a LOT lesson and will help you to manage the session more effectively.

Travelling to venues

Learners should be aware when they enrol on the course that they may be expected to use public transport during a lesson, but it is advisable to remind them of this when they begin studying. A student, for example, must not be allowed to hold up the rest of the group because they do not possess a valid ticket.

It is very important that students know where they are going for each stage of the lesson, at what time, and how they will be getting there. The chief reason for this is that if at any stage an individual becomes separated from the group they are able to make their own way to the next meeting place without any cause for panic. Students should always be aware of the route they are taking when travelling, in order that they are able to retrace it alone if necessary.

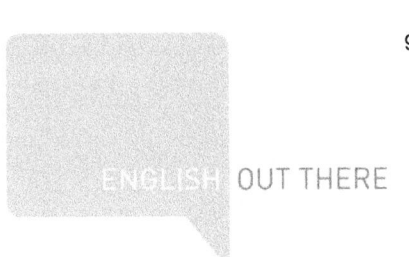

In a café or bar

We strongly recommend that teachers inform each group that they should not buy refreshments during the first two stages of the lesson and that there is a natural break at the end of the activity stage, when drinks can be taken. Learners should also be clearly informed that when the third stage of the lesson is held in a cafe or bar, they would be expected to buy a soft drink/tea or coffee.

In preparation for the final stage in a cafe it is advisable that the teacher visits this venue in advance to assess the seating arrangements. Tables can be put together and chairs found before the group arrives. With large groups in particular this can save time and confusion.

Meeting up

The group **should not** wait for students who do not turn up at the specified meeting place at the allotted time and students must be made aware of this in advance. Given the nature of the lessons and how they are organised, it is important that no time is wasted and students must take responsibility for this and work within the time limits specified.

Breaks

Some learners may be concerned about the lack of allocated breaks during the lesson. Conversely, other students may be concerned about the time taken up travelling to venues. These two opposing concerns answer each other – the break times are spent travelling, and give the class an opportunity to relax and chat to each other. The planning of this prior to the lesson by the teacher means that the students do not have to worry about getting to the venue and can actually relax.

Contingency plans Out There

We have already discussed the importance of planning lessons, timing, travel and the venue carefully. However, sometimes situations arise that are outside your control. While these cannot be avoided, there are certain provisions that can be put in place to minimise the disruption caused.

Weather

Inclement weather is a fact of life, and students should be aware that coats and umbrellas are essential in some countries! Likewise, sunglasses, sunscreen and hats are a good idea when classes are spending time outside with questionnaires.

Travel

It is a good idea for teachers to plan alternative routes to a venue, for example both by bus and train. This prepares them in the event of public transport disruption

Venue closures

One of the worst case scenarios for a teacher is finding a venue shut, or an exhibition closed to the public. Smaller museums can suffer staff shortages, and exhibits can sometimes be closed when cleaning is in progress or a private group has booked the venue. As always, check the venue as close to the time of visiting as possible. Try to have as a back up another venue or an activity worksheet that is not dependent on the venue. For example, a visit to a famous house to look rooms and furniture could be substituted by a visit to the furniture department of a large department store. Alternatively, a venue day can always be turned into a speaking day with an improvised questionnaire.

The group becomes separated

In a busy city this is always a risk if the group is not managed properly. See the section on Class Management for ways to avoid this. Always make sure that the group know where they are going and how to get back to the school. Teachers with mobile phones should contact the school and make the office aware of the situation.

Stage three location

The third stage of the lesson takes place in a cafe, park or other public space. There is no reason why these areas, if thoroughly researched, tested and selected, should not be as effective as a formal classroom.

Where cafes and bars are being used, it is worth talking to the manager to see if an arrangement can be made regarding the use of a function room or quiet area.

Museums and galleries often have education rooms available, and these may need booking in advance.

Venues must:

- be within a short walk of the activity venue.
- have seating and writing facilities.
- not be too noisy.

Key rules to remember when asking the public questions

While individuals usually respond best to questions directly relating to themselves and their experiences, they should never be asked anything inappropriately personal or intrusive.

In the same way that a teacher wanting to start a class discussion will introduce a topic gradually, to prepare the class and start them thinking, the public also need to be 'warmed up' if we are to obtain interesting and rewarding responses.

It is advisable that the first couple of questions are designed with this in mind, and if you create your own questionnaires (which you might want to do at higher levels), should never dive straight in with the 'heavy' questions. In any case, once the teacher has started designing questionnaires they will find out for themselves the format that produces the best results.

The group must be taught how to approach members of the public. Before leaving the classroom the group should pre-teach and drill the following introduction:

'Excuse me, I'm learning English. Could I ask you a few questions please?'

It is important that each learner feels comfortable and confident with this opening line, and lower levels should be individually drilled as well as chorally.

Lower levels may benefit from some other very useful phrases in their own right, such as 'Could you speak a little more slowly please?', 'Could you repeat that please?', and 'How do you spell that?'

When the group go out with their questionnaires it is important to think about the group dynamics. Some learners may prefer to be alone; others feel more confident with a partner. Sometimes it works well to pair an experienced, confident student with a shyer one; at other times quieter students paired up become more vocal.

There are variations on the way a questionnaire is conducted. Usually the learner asks the questions and writes down the answers. Depending on the aim, there may be more productive alternatives. One option is to pair up the students and one asks while the other writes. They should then swap roles for the next interview. This permits a more natural exchange between learner and respondent, and can allow a discussion to take place rather than a question-answer scenario. In the same way, students may benefit from being asked not to write anything down at all. Where specific language structures are being practiced, a tighter framework is preferable, while a looser style is more appropriate where opinions are being sought.

Mobile phones can now record sound and video and, if the person being interviewed agrees, there is no harm in trying to record the sessions for later analysis.

Class management

Stage one - input

Pace of the lesson

A LOT lesson is faster paced than a conventional classroom-based lesson, for a number of reasons.

- There is less of a drive towards maximising student talking time in stages one (and three). The second stage of the lesson gives the learners plenty of opportunity for speaking hence the first stage must focus far more on structured activities and input.
- Each lesson is self-contained. Timing and planning are crucial to ensure that the lesson *is* completed.
- Given the structure of the lesson, each stage is dependent upon the other stages. Stage two will not be possible if stage one has not been completed first, since the learners will not have the required language or motivation to complete the activity either in the real world or online. In the same way, learners will not be able to achieve the intended result if they have not collected the information in the activity stage. Additionally, each stage has a rigid time limit within that particular lesson plan. There is no possibility to run over if the stage is not completed in the time allocated. If a teacher runs out of time, the overall task and aim of the lesson is difficult to achieve.

Accuracy versus fluency

- As discussed above, the second stage invariably provides the fluency practice. Whilst the teacher will observe, monitor and assist where necessary, the object of the second stage is not accuracy. The object is exposure to and practice of the language. For this reason there must be an emphasis during the first (and third) stage on input and accuracy. In this respect the lessons are a departure from the traditional classroom procedure of maximising learner talking time at every opportunity, often at the expense of accuracy.

Stage two - activity

Teachers of conventional lessons may not be used to taking groups of students out of the classroom and might have some logistical and safety concerns.

Teachers whose students are using *VoIP* for real practice should make sure that there are sufficient computers available for the class in the school or that their students have online access at home. Here are a few pointers that will make management of the group more efficient when they are being taken out of the classroom into the real world.

Before leaving the classroom

- Make sure each individual knows where they are going, how they are getting there and how long they are staying
- Make it clear to learners that the group will not wait for anyone who fails to keep up, or fails to meet at the designated meeting place, or at the designated time.
- Never set off for the venue until you have head-counted the group and allow them a few minutes to prepare themselves.
- The travelling time (whether walking, taking the bus etc.) should be no more than 20 minutes and this time is effectively the students' break time. Encourage them to use this time to get to know each other and relax. It is a good opportunity for teachers to get to know their students also.
- En route

- Keep the pace fast and mingle with the group to ensure everyone is encouraged to keep up.
- Periodically stop and regroup. This is especially important before catching trains and buses.

On arrival at the venue

- On arrival, gather in a quiet area before you disperse the group to carry out their task. This should be in same area that you expect them to reconvene on completion of the activity or outside the café or bar chosen for stage three.
- Check that everyone understands the task.
- Pair or group students if necessary.
- Make sure each learner is aware of the time they should reconvene – ask them to repeat it back to you.
- Tell the group where the third stage will be held. (Although you expect the group to meet in the designated place and go together to the selected area for the third stage of the lesson, this permits a student to catch up with the group if a problem arises which delays them.)

During the activity

The group will disperse to complete the activity. You should walk around monitoring the individuals, both to be on hand if they have any problems or queries and to ensure that they are completing the activity correctly. You might like to set boundaries in larger locations to keep the group in a smaller area to make monitoring them easier.

Stage three - result

Classes practising online can either reconvene in a classroom after the activity session or at the next scheduled class session. As discussed earlier, real world activities require some planning of the stage three locations.

The stage three locations are likely to be public areas such as cafes or parks. Depending on the task and the venue, it may be more effective to divide the class into groups or pairs, so that the teacher can move around and talk to smaller groups rather than attempt to address the group as a whole.

Certain venues will lend themselves better to certain activities than others. A cafe, for example, will provide tables and chairs but also the possibility of some background noise. It therefore lends itself to a writing task. A park, with no tables and chairs but peace and privacy is ideal for oral presentations and role-plays.

As in stage one, the emphasis in this session must be on accuracy rather than fluency. Students have had the second hour to use the language relatively freely, and will now need correction and re-formulation.

Exit questionnaires

Feedback from learners on all aspects of their experience is vital. If you use LOT lessons to create a practical short course, the day before their course is due to end learners should receive an exit questionnaire (see below), which they complete and hand in before they leave. Do please take notice of the comments on questionnaires and forward examples to us from time to time. We really like to receive all feedback from you and your students.

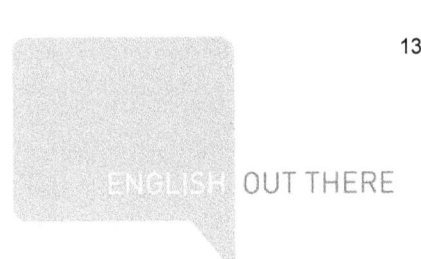

Appendix 1: Languages Out There placement test

Student name: _____   Date: _____   Level: _____

Interview Questions

Ask students questions from the list and mark the **understanding** and the **answers** given:

0 is given when a question is not understood, 1 for beginner competency, going up to 6 for Advanced.

a. Where do you live and what do you do?	0 1 2 3 4 5 6
b. How do you get to school?	0 1 2 3 4 5 6
c. Tell me about yourself. For example, what do you do?	0 1 2 3 4 5 6
d. Do you have any hobbies? Can you tell me about them?	0 1 2 3 4 5 6
e. Can you describe your house or flat? Can you describe your room to me please?	0 1 2 3 4 5 6
f. What's your favourite type of music? Can you describe it?	0 1 2 3 4 5 6
g. What countries would you like to visit? Why?	0 1 2 3 4 5 6
h. What are your future plans?	0 1 2 3 4 5 6
i. If you won the lottery what would you do?	0 1 2 3 4 5 6
j. If you hadn't decided to study English, what other language would have studied and why?	0 1 2 3 4 5 6
Situation tasks (if the average mark of the above answers is above 2 choose one of the situation tasks below (the list starts with easy tasks and finishes with the most difficult)	0 1 2 3 4 5 6
❏ You are in a restaurant. You'd like to order fish and chips. What do you say?	
❏ You are asking for directions to a railway station. A lady tells you to turn right at the 'crossroads'. You do not understand 'crossroads'. What do you say?	
❏ Your friend asked you to help him get a gift for their teacher. What do you say? What do you suggest?	
❏ Someone has telephoned to speak to your colleague about something important. However, your colleague is not there. What do you say to the caller?	
❏ You bought a bag yesterday, and it is broken. You take it back to the shop. What do you say?	
❏ You are in a bank, trying to withdraw cash from a cash-point. The machine swallows your card. What do you do or say?	
❏ A friend asked you to describe your favourite film in one sentence. What do you say?	

Comments:

Appendix 2:

Welcome to _____

Your class will be in (enter room number and building name):

Your building number, Street name, **Your town, postcode** What do you need? A pen and notebook Money for a drink or a snack A travel pass	If you have any problems or questions: 1- You can ask your teacher. 2- You can ask ……….. the course manager in room (x). 3- Your teacher's mobile phone number is (enter number) 4- If you have an emergency- call: **(enter number)**

Your LOT class will be in 3 parts.

- Part 1   80 mins.   In the classroom with your teacher.
  Travel Out There
- Part 2   40 mins   *Out There Task* in the street, museum, gallery, etc.
  Meet your class
- Part 3   40 mins   Feedback, usually in a café (you must buy a drink or a snack).

- Make sure your **mobile phone** is switched **off** for the entire three hour period - even travelling is part of the lesson.
- The *Out There* part is a very important part of the lesson. You are outside to do your task. Not to go sightseeing or shopping!!!
- Please note that your teacher is **not** there to give you a **guided tour** of the *Out There* location. They will accompany you *Out There* and will be around if you need help and assistance, but then you will be paired up to go about the tasks.
- Please do not buy food or drinks during the first 2 hours of the lesson. You should be working hard in this time and should save your money for the **third part**, when class **will be in a café**, and it is polite to **buy** a small bottle of water or a **tea or coffee** (and you will be thirsty!).
- The first part will provide you with the language you will need to complete the tasks in the *Out There* part, and it is therefore vital that you **arrive on time**. Students arriving more than ten minutes late may not be allowed into the classroom.

If you have any questions or problems with any of the above, or with any other aspect of your course, please talk to your teacher, who will be happy to help you.

Enjoy your class.

Day to day checklist - before entering the classroom
Have you got...?
- Lesson plan?
- Enough copies of task-sheets, questionnaires and pictures?
- Directions to the venues for stages 2 and 3?
- Names of learners
- Board markers, pens and paper?
- Enthusiasm and a smile?

Before leaving the classroom
Have you informed each individual...?
- Where they are going, how they are getting there and how long they are staying?
- That the group will not wait for anyone who fails to keep up, or fails to meet in the designated meeting place, or fails to meet at the designated time.

Before starting the activity
Have you...?
- Checked that everyone understands the task?
- Paired or grouped learners if necessary?
- Made sure each learner is aware of the time they should reconvene?
- Told the group where the third stage will be held in case they miss the rendezvous?

Leaving questionnaire:

Thank you for choosing to study with us using LOT materials. We hope you enjoyed your course and most importantly, that you have learnt a lot.

We really want to know what you think about the school, so please take a few minutes to answer the questions below.

Name (optional) _____   Age: _____
Nationality: _____   Email: _____
Level _____   Teacher _____
Length of Course: _____   Date: _____

1. How did you hear about the course?

2. Did you enjoy using the LOT materials and learning *Out There*? (comment on reasons)

3. Now that you have finished, was the school/course what you expected before you started?

    1. Please circle ○ a number: **1 = ☹ 3 = 😐 5 = ☺**

a. Learning English   1 2 3 4 5
b. Enjoying lessons   1 2 3 4 5
c. Cost of the course   1 2 3 4 5
d. Advice and help   1 2 3 4 5

5. Is there anything else you want to tell us?

6. Would you recommend us to a friend?   Yes/No

7. Can we use this information on our website/promotional materials? Yes/No

                    Thank you. We hope to see you again soon!

Instructions for language school learners using *VoIP* (i.e. Skype, Google Talk, Messenger or a voice enabled social network) for practice:

These instructions will help you to make the most of your language lessons as you study at the language school using the LOT materials.

- Make contact with some fluent or native speakers via **Skype or** an online language exchange like www.italki.com, www.livemocha.com, www.mylanguageexchange.com, www.myngle.com, www.babbel.com or www.language-exchanges.org or through Skype language learning forums .
- Make initial contact with them by text, video or voice mail, this is polite before you call someone; even if you can see they are online. In the message tell them what you want to talk about (i.e. the lesson 'topic') and say it will only take a few minutes.
- **It's a good idea to make friends with quite a few people around the world in different time zones. If you have fifteen or twenty friendly practice partners you will find that one or more will be online and happy to talk when you want to do some practice. Tell them that you want to practise with them and that it will only take a few minutes each time you call them and that they don't need to do any preparation to have the conversation. When you contact them tell them what you want to talk about (i.e. the lesson 'topic').**
- Attend your class and use the materials your teacher gives you.
- When your teacher tells you, either use the computers in the school or use your own computer, to call your conversation partners.
- Make sure you understand the final *Out There* task.
- Try to relax…
- Call one of your *Out There* conversation partners and practice the language you have just studied.
- Record it and listen again, then call other *Out There* conversation partners for further practice.

Complete the whole task and use your partners to cover all of the language in the lesson but feel free to talk about other subjects with them once you have covered the language in the lesson; and most of all have fun and get to know your partners well. They are there to help you improve your English.

Lesson Plan

Level 4	Topic	Aim	Language Focus	Skills
Lesson 1	My city	To get recommendations for activities in a city	Recommending, suggesting and vocabulary for activities	Reading, speaking, listening

Out There – real world	*Out There* – VoIP
Take students to a place where people are hanging out and not in a rush. They are generally more approachable if they are sitting down. Think parks, squares and civic spaces where people take a break from their busy day.	Tell students to use VoIP to call conversation partners using the school's computers or at home.

#	Details	Task Sheet	Minutes
1	To introduce the aim and task of the day, tell the class that you have to organise weekend activities for friends coming to visit your city. Ask the students to recommend something. Write their answers on the board, highlighting corrected mistakes, and introduce the task of the day.		10
2	Elicit suggestions and make a list on the board of ways of asking for recommendations, e.g. 'Can you recommend any activities for a group or for old school friends?' Include ways of recommending/suggesting, e.g. 'You should go to the pub,' or phrases such as 'what you want to do is…', 'the best is…', '… is good for…', 'I think… is the best…'	1	10
3	Pre-reading activity: without explaining new vocabulary, ask the students to look at the groups of people and think about what they would like to do. Students discuss in pairs and match the categories to the ones in the article. Check their answers, go through new vocabulary and ask them to do Exercise 2. Check in open class.	2	30
4	Ask the students to work in pairs and suggest activities for the 13 categories from the article. Monitor and help with pronunciation.	3	10
5	Read 'Tomorrow's world' to see if the students' suggestions match the ones in the text. After reading ask the students to make a summary of the text.	4	10
6	Explain the *Out There* task: ask the students to prepare questions and write them on the questionnaire sheet. Give suggestions, check accuracy of new questions and check intonation.		10

	Out There Tasks		
7	**Real world:** Students ask members of the public their questions to start conversations.	**VoIP:** Students ask conversation partners their questions to start conversations.	40
8	**Feedback:** Ask how it went. Check the students have completed the task. Ask them to list their favourite new expressions and words of the day. Ask if they feel confident with the language taught and get feedback.	**Feedback:** Same as real world when in class, but also think about having students do the task as homework, record it and email it to you as an assessment.	45

© 2007/2008 Languages Out There and its licensors. Reproduction in whole or in part prohibited except as may be provided under the terms of a Licence Agreement. www.languagesoutthere.com

Task Sheet 1

Exercise 1

Pre-reading: look at these groups of people. You will match them to activities in the text, what do you think they would like to do?

- somebody who likes ghosts
- a group of guys
- somebody who likes new things
- couples
- homosexuals
- a group of girls
- a classy person.
- somebody who doesn't want to spend much money
- somebody who likes museums
- food lovers
- children
- fashion victims
- somebody with unusual or crazy taste or personality

When you finish reading check your answers with your partner.

Exercise 2

Use some of the words/phrases below to fill the gaps. Make the necessary changes to fit the sentences:

the charm	to ditch something/body	action-packed (adj.)	to break the bank
to be spoilt for choice	loopy (adj.)	eccentric (adj.)	cutting-edge (adj.)
lad	A gastropub		

a. It's not very traditional, it's a _____. You know, one of these places that serves fancy beers and gourmet food. Are you coming with us?

b. He's not a child any more, he's a fine young _____!

c. This is great, there is so much to choose from, ____ _____ _____ _____ _____!

d. I think he's going _____, he's acting very strange.

e. It only costs £2. That's not going to _____ _____ _____.

Now use the other five words or expressions and make examples:

f.

g.

h.

j.

k.

Task Sheet 2

London Calling
Here are some ideas for things to do in a large city – in this case London

Second Honeymoon?
What could be better than a romantic weekend in London? We've got it covered.

Culture Vulture
Calling all culture lovers - London has inspirational art, theatre and heritage galore.

Ditch the Diet!
Many gastronomic delights await you in London from the finest restaurants to gourmet markets.

Girls Just Want to Have Fun
Everything you need for the perfect girly getaway - so what are you waiting for?

Boys Will Be Boys
Enjoy an action-packed weekend away with the lads; you may even need a holiday afterwards to recover!

On a Budget
There's so much to see and do in London without breaking the bank, you'll be simply spoilt for choice.

Carry On Camping
Everything the gay visitor could wish for: fantastic restaurants, the best clubs, world class fashion and more!

Loopy London
Fancy something a bit eccentric? London is one of the most excitingly unpredictable places you could visit.

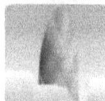
Tomorrow's World
London is among the most cutting-edge cities in the world so take some time to explore its modern side.

Passion for Fashion
Calling all fashionistas! This the perfect weekend for you - and a perhaps a pal or two.

High Spirits
Scare yourself silly with a weekend full of haunted hotels, dreadful dungeons, twilight tours and ghostly gastropubs.

Lounge Lizard
The epitome of charm and sophistication, our bar and lounge lizard knows how to do London in style!

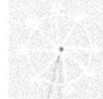
Big Kids
Feed the kid within! From magical entertainment and thrill rides to a school disco - you certainly won't be bored.

Task Sheet 3

Tomorrow's world

Old London Town, they call it. And there's no doubt about it – the cathedrals, museums, bridges and cobbled streets of the capital are a nostalgist's dream come true. But the name is slightly misleading too: London is also one of the most cutting-edge cities in the world.

With award-winning skyscrapers, the futuristic new Wembley Stadium set for completion in the spring of 2007, bars and clubs that look like the cantina in Star Wars and fashions that are five years ahead of the game – not to mention the rapid progress being made towards building a whole new 'city' for the 2012 Olympic Games, London is rapidly becoming Buck Rogers' kind of place. Here are a few tips to help you plan ahead – in more ways than one:

- **The BIG picture** - find out what it's like to walk in space by catching Magnificent Desolation: Walking on the Moon in eye-popping 3D at the bfi London IMAX. The UK's biggest cinema screen, it's roughly the height of five double-decker buses.

- **Voyage of discovery** - you won't quite reach the speed of light aboard a London RIB (rigid inflatable boat) as you power along the Thames, but it'll feel like it.

- **Brilliant buildings** - check out millennial masterpieces of architecture like the gherkin-shaped, curved-glass 30 St Mary Axe, London's new City Hall (home to Mayor Ken Livingstone) and Britain's tallest building, 1 Canada Square, at Canary Wharf.

- **But is it art** - delve into some of the world's most forward-thinking minds at Tate Modern or the Design Museum.

- **Get an Eye pod** - try your best to eat while your jaw drops at the panoramic views, glass ceilings and swivel chairs of Plateau, located on the 4th floor of Canada Place.

- **Eye in the sky** - take a ride on the *2001: A Space Odyssey*-like British Airways London Eye. The power it takes to revolve once is equivalent to around six light bulbs per person.

- **Weird science** - get your hands on some of the 300,000 exhibits at the Science Museum. Check out the events programme for the museum's Dana Centre too – a cool venue complete with bar which hosts fascinating events and debates.

Out There Task

Real world - to start your conversation, say to people: 'Excuse me, I am learning English. Can I ask you some questions please?' If you work in pairs one should speak while the other writes. Swap roles for the next person you speak to. Talk to at least four people each.

VoIP – call conversation partners and ask them your questions to start a conversation. Ask them about the place where they live. Remember you can record your conversation to listen to later.

Create your own questions. Ask for activity recommendations for different groups of people.

Q1.-

Q2.-

Q3.-

Q4.-

Q5.-

Notes

Lesson Plan

Level 4	Topic	Aim	Language Focus	Skills
Lesson 2	Observation - people and events	To describe people and what they were doing	Past continuous, past simple and appearance, adjectives of description	Speaking, listening

Out There – real world	*Out There* – VoIP
In a gallery or a place near the school, like a park or a riverside, where people are passing by jogging, cycling, roller-skating, walking etc.	Tell students to use VoIP to call conversation partners on the school's computers or at home.

#	Details	Task Sheet	Minutes
1	To introduce the aim and task of the day briefly show a picture of somebody doing something and ask the students to remember what they see. Hide the picture and ask the students to describe the person and what was happening. Write what they say on the board, highlight any mistakes to be corrected, and explain the aim of the lesson		10
2	Ask class: 'If you need to describe somebody, what are the important aspects?' Elicit e.g. colour/type of hair, height, build, complexion, scars, tattoos, beard. Write items of vocabulary on the board and ask the students to copy in their task sheet space.	1	15
3	Describe someone famous for your students to guess. Then tell them to write a description of somebody internationally famous for their partner to guess. Check in open class and give points for correct guesses.	1	15
4	Explain the difference between past simple ('they ran out of the bank') and past continuous ('they were wearing masks'). One action happened in the middle of the other. Draw the timeline and ask the students to copy it. Write the form and elicit examples using both verbs in each sentence.	2	10
5	Say to the class: 'There's been a robbery.' They are witnesses. They need to describe what they saw to the police. Ask them to look at the scene of the robbery for three minutes, then turn it over and write what they remember. What was happening? Monitor and help with tenses.		15
6	Review what each pair remembered and what was happening.		10
7	Explain the *Out There* task.		5
	Out There Tasks		
8	**Real world:** Observe and describe people, in pictures in a gallery or outside. Observe what people were doing in as much detail as possible.	**VoIP:** Tell students to use VoIP to call some conversation partners.	40
9	**Feedback:** Ask how it went. Check the students have completed the task. Ask them to list their favourite new expressions and words of the day. Ask if they feel confident with the language taught and get feedback.	**Feedback:** Same as real world when in class, but also think about having students do the task as homework, record it and email it to you as an assessment.	45

© 2007/2008 Languages Out There and its licensors. Reproduction in whole or in part prohibited except as may be provided under the terms of a Licence Agreement. www.languagesoutthere.com

Task Sheet 1

1. Describing people's appearance:

Vocabulary

2. Describe somebody internationally famous. Don't say who it is, your classmates have to guess. Don't make it too easy:

Task Sheet 2

1. Past simple and past continuous:

Past_____Now

2. What were you doing:

at 7:00 this morning
at 10:30 last night
at 4:00 this morning
this time last week
last Tuesday
last summer
on your last holiday

Task Sheet 3

Out There Task

1. Observe people and what is going on around you. Imagine you have taken a photograph of what you see.

Describe the people, what they looked like, what was happening and what they were doing. Give as much detail as possible, as if you were a witness to a crime scene. Use vocabulary from the lesson and past continuous.

Or, in an art gallery, find at least four paintings that show human figures doing something or find people in the gallery doing something.

Out There Task

2. Visit a website like www.images.google.co.uk and search for something like 'sporting people' - you will see lots of pictures of active people.

Send the URL as a text to your partner. When you are both looking at the same web page describe the people pictured to your conversation partner and also what they were doing when the photo was taken. Ask them to guess which picture.
Then ask your conversation partner to describe a person and what they were doing when the photo was taken. Write down what they say.

Ask your conversation partners these questions and write down their answers.
What do you look like?

What were you doing at this time last week?

What were you doing at this time last year?

What does your best friend look like?

What were you doing last time you were together?

Lesson Plan

Level 4	Topic	Aim	Language Focus	Skills
Lesson 3	Manners	To discuss differences in manners between individuals and nationalities	Idioms and phrases used to give opinions	Reading, speaking, listening

Out There – real world	*Out There* – VoIP
Take students to a place where people are hanging out and not in a rush. They are generally more approachable if they are sitting down. Think parks, squares and civic spaces where people take a break from their busy day.	Tell students to call conversation partners using VoIP.

#	Details	Task Sheet	Minutes
1	To introduce the aim of the lesson and the task, as the class come in and settle, do a few things that could be construed as being 'bad manners'. Such as closing the door in someone's face, kicking someone's bag in the floor or picking your nose. Monitor their reactions and then ask them what is wrong. Try to elicit the phrase 'bad manners'. Explain the aim of the lesson.		10
2	Pre-reading: ask the students to think of experiences of both good and bad manners and list them on the board. Hand out the article and ask the students to read the introduction and compare to the list on the board.	1	10
3	In pairs, one student reads interviews 1-2-3 from the article, the other reads 4-5-6, then they exchange information. As a class discussion, ask the students which of the views they agree with.		15
4	Students do matching exercise on idioms from the article (key: 1. d; 2. e; 3. g; 4. i; 5.a; 6.h; 7.b; 8. c; 9. j; 10. k; 11.f.) and ask the students to make examples using the idioms.	2	20
5	Go through phrases for expressing opinion from the article and add others. Work though new vocabulary and drill.		10
6	Discuss the point made in the article and students' own opinions. Ask them to think of what is considered good or bad manners in their country – compare and discuss in class. Encourage use of the new lexis.		10
7	Explain the *Out There* task. Drill the questions and go through possible answers.	3	5

Out There Tasks		
8	**Real world:** Students ask members of the public their questions to start conversations.	**VoIP:** Students ask conversation partners their questions to start conversations.	40
9	**Feedback:** Ask how it went. Check the students have completed the task. Ask them to list their favourite new expressions and words of the day. Ask if they feel confident with the language taught and get feedback.	**Feedback:** Same as real world when in class, but also think about having students do the task as homework, record it and email it to you as an assessment.	45

© 2007/2008 Languages Out There and its licensors. Reproduction in whole or in part prohibited except as may be provided under the terms of a Licence Agreement. www.languagesoutthere.com

Task Sheet 1

Manners today

Introduction
Are people today less polite than they used to be? You often hear people, particularly elderly people, complaining that people today are ill-mannered compared with 'the old days'. For example, people no longer give up their seat on a train to old people or mothers with young children. Men don't hold doors open for women. People eat and smoke on the street and kiss each other in public. Fifty years ago such behaviour would have been unimaginable. But are the modern generation really ruder than their grandparents? Here are some people talking about manners today:

1. Eric
"I think things are less formal these days but I quite like that, I have to say. In the old days people had to wear a suit and tie to the office but **these days** it seems that **anything goes**. I wear jeans and a t-shirt and no-one **bats an eyelid**. I think it's **down to** a change in attitudes, especially in attitudes towards people in authority. **In my view** people are less willing to be pushed around by their so-called superiors. That's the way I see it, anyway."

2. Lisa
"Things are definitely different nowadays, but that doesn't mean they're worse. People are much busier these days and they don't have time for all the social niceties that preoccupied people in the past. Sure, people eat and drink in the street but what's wrong with that? It's perfectly normal. **I wouldn't say** it was bad manners. It's more a case of convenience."

3. Paul
"Of course things are different these days but I don't think it's a question of bad manners. **In my view, it's all down to** equality. Women expect equal treatment these days and if I offer a seat to a woman or open a door for her she might easily get offended. Women should buy their own drinks too!"

4. Ken
"The only thing I can't stand is people kissing in the street. **I can't stand that**. Why should I have to watch them?"

5. Drew
"The thing that drives me mad these days is noise. Not just the noise of the traffic. I can **put up with** that. It's things like people playing music at full volume or using their mobile phone on the train when I'm trying to read. My neighbours are always doing DIY at the weekend – banging, drilling and so on so you **can hardly hear yourself think**. But worst of all are the dogs. My other neighbour's got three and they bark all the time. It **drives me mad**!"

6. Anne
"Some people try and **make out** that we're all rude these days but **I don't see it like that.** Drivers usually stop for pedestrians at zebra crossings, don't they? And most people will politely wait their turn in a queue without trying to push in at the front. Sure, a lot of people are aggressive, especially when they're driving but **at the end of the day** I think **on the whole** things are all right."

Task Sheet 2

A. Some idioms and other phrases from the article - match them with their meaning:

1.	it drives me mad	a.	it's because of/due to
2.	I wouldn't say	b.	I really don't like
3.	these days	c.	it's very noisy
4.	I don't see it like that	d.	it makes me really angry
5.	It's all down to	e.	I don't think
6.	anything goes	f.	generally
7.	I can't stand	g.	now
8.	you can hardly hear yourself think	h.	everything is possible
9.	no-one bats an eyelid	i.	I don't agree
10.	to make out (one of its meanings)	j.	no-one cares or is offended
11.	on the whole	k.	to claim

B. Make examples using the idioms and phrases from above:

1. _____
2. _____
3. _____
4. _____
5. _____
6. _____
7. _____
8. _____
9. _____
10. _____
11. _____

Out There Task

Real world - to start your conversation, say to people: "Excuse me, I am learning English. Can I ask you some questions please?" If you work in pairs, one person should speak while the other writes. Swap roles for the next person you speak to. Talk to at least four people each.

VoIP – Call conversation partners and ask them these questions to start a conversation. Remember you can record your conversation to listen to later.

What do you think about people jumping queues? Why?

What about people kissing on the streets? Why?

What about someone swearing in public? Why?

What about someone speaking loudly on the phone in public? Why?

Do you think people are more or less polite now? Why?

What other examples of good or bad manners do you see?

© 2007/2008 Languages Out There and its licensors. Reproduction in whole or in part prohibited except as may be provided under the terms of a Licence Agreement. www.languagesoutthere.com

Lesson Plan

Level 4	Topic	Aim	Language Focus	Skills
Lesson 4	Technology and possibilities	To enable students to discuss future possibilities	Modals of probability, possibility and certainty	Reading, writing speaking, listening

Out There – real world	*Out There* – VoIP
Take the class to a well-populated area of the town or city, somewhere where people are not in a rush and are easy to approach (i.e. sitting down).	Tell students to call conversation partners using VoIP.

#	Details	Task Sheet	Minutes
1	To introduce the aim and task of the day, tell the class about something currently big in the news. Ask students what they think will happen and encourage them to use expressions like 'I reckon/probably' or modals of probability (e.g. 'I reckon the MP3 will be superseded by another form of playing music, as with vinyl records and CD's.').		5
2	Task Sheet 1: In pairs students rearrange the sentences expressing possibility and certainty and go through them. Students check with other pairs and discuss. Check in open class.	1	15
3	Hand out Task Sheet 2 and make sure students are clear about the answers/rules. Discuss possibility and certainty and modals of probability and possibility. Students create two sentences each - one expressing probability and one of possibility. Feedback and correction to class.	2	20
4	Ask students to change the level of certainty in the sentences by using different modals/adverbs/verbs, e.g. '(8) In fifty years time machines will possibly govern our lives'. Alternatively, students make their own examples using the new language.		10
5	Task Sheet 3: reading. Ask the students to read the text carefully and fill the gaps using the six phrases at the beginning. Discuss some of the ideas in the text. Do they agree with the writer's opinions about the technological future?	3	15
6	Explain the *Out There* task. Students make questions about the future of the various topics and discuss possible answers.	4	10

Out There Tasks		
7	**Real world:** Students ask members of the public their questions to start conversations.	**VoIP:** Students ask conversation partners their questions to start conversations.	40
8	**Feedback:** Ask how it went. Check the students have completed the task. Ask them to list their favourite new expressions and words of the day. Ask if they feel confident with the language taught and get feedback.	**Feedback:** Same as real world when in class, but also think about having students do the task as homework, record it and email it to you as an assessment.	45

© 2007/2008 Languages Out There and its licensors. Reproduction in whole or in part prohibited except as may be provided under the terms of a Licence Agreement. www.languagesoutthere.com

Task Sheet 1

Possibility and certainty

Look at the sentences and try to put the words into the correct order:

1. shopping on people definitely do most will of the internet their
2. will probably videophone have everyone a
3. smaller mobile get and computers will smaller and phones
4. replace money electronic will probably transactions
5. effect on this certainly have an human will interaction
6. and more people will more home work at
7. protect the the the may government individual have to privacy of
8. in machines years time will fifty completely lives govern our

Write your answers here:

1.

2.

3.

4.

5.

6.

7.

8.

Task Sheet 2

Possibility and certainty

Look at these sentences. Circle all the words expressing possibility. Then circle all the words expressing certainty:

1. People will definitely do most of their shopping on the internet.
2. Everyone will probably have a videophone.
3. Mobile phones and computers will get smaller and smaller.
4. Electronic transactions will probably replace money.
5. This will certainly have an effect on human interaction.
6. More and more people will work at home.
7. The government may have to protect the privacy of the individual.
8. In fifty years time machines will completely govern our lives.

Which of the circled words are modal verbs?

And which are adverbs?

What is their position in the sentence?

Write your changed sentences below:

1.
2.
3.
4.
5.
6.
7.
8.

Task Sheet 3

Fill the gaps in the text using these phrases:

- work at home
- on the internet
- human interaction
- smaller and smaller
- protect the privacy
- replace money

What is our society going to look like in fifty years' time? What with amazing advances in technology and medicine, not to mention the globalisation of trade and information, it seems to me that the world is about to enter a new technological age.

I think that the most important scientific advance in our time is the computer. Computers have automated uncountable operations in our daily lives. For example, rather than travelling to the bank, people will do their banking on the internet. Electronic financial transactions will probably _____ _____. I also think that people will definitely do most of their shopping _____ _____. Nowadays you can buy just about anything online, from cars to houses.

Also, as a result of the internet's networking capability, more and more people will _____ _____. Virtual offices are becoming more and more popular, because the absence of a physical office cuts overheads significantly. In addition to this, everyone will probably have a video phone or will use video conferencing over the internet. Mobile phones and computers will also get _____ _____, making them increasingly portable. Furthermore, with the massive increase in online communities and chat software, including MSN Messenger, Yahoo Messenger and Skype, people are spending more time at home having virtual relationships online. I believe this will certainly have an effect on _____ _____.

The internet is a very open network, which makes it vulnerable to hackers and others who want to invade the privacy of those who use it. In response to this I think that the government may have to _____ _____ of the individual. In order to do this, they will have to monitor the usage of the internet more strictly.

I can't help thinking that in fifty years time machines will completely govern our lives.

Out There Task

Real world – To start your conversation, first say to people: "Excuse me, I am learning English. Can I ask you some questions please?" If you work in pairs one person should speak while the other writes. Swap roles for the next person you speak to. Talk to at least four people each.

VoIP – Call conversation partners and ask them these questions to start a conversation. Remember you can record your conversation to listen to later.

internet shopping

videophones

mobile phones

electronic money

working from home

machines replacing people

Notes

Lesson Plan

Level 4	Topic	Aim	Language Focus	Skills
Lesson 5	Shopping	To find and describe items	Shopping vocabulary, comparatives/ superlatives	Speaking, listening

Out There – real world	Out There – VoIP
A department store or large shop.	Tell students to use VoIP to call conversation partners using the school's computers or at home

#	Details	Task Sheet	Minutes
1	To introduce the aim and task of the day, tell the class about your latest purchase (e.g. 'I bought this top in a shopping centre. It cost £10.99. While I was there I saw an offer – two for £20 – and I bought them too'.). Explain any unknown expressions and tell the class about today's task.		5
2	What things have you bought recently? Tell students to find a partner and to tell them.		10
3	Task Sheet 1: ask the students to work in pairs to discuss when they last bought the items listed in the box. Discuss in open class.	1	15
4	Vocabulary: students find the names of various shops. Check in open class. Check pronunciation.		10
5	Students decide who would say the phrases in a shop: a customer or an assistant.		10
6	Introduce comparatives and superlatives: present and practice the language using prices of different products as examples. Demonstrate form comparing two items then superlatives with a third.	2	15
7	Role-play: ask the students to make a dialogue using shopping phrases, using the prompts in the box. Then they change the details to create their own role-play.		10
8	Explain the *Out There* task.		5

	Out There Tasks		
9	**Real world:** Students find items in a department store to describe and compare. **Feedback:**	**VoIP:** Students write descriptions of items from an online store and then describe them to their conversation partners before comparing them with other similar items.	40
10	Ask how it went and check the students have completed the task. Ask them to list their favourite new expressions and words of the day and whether they feel confident with the language taught. Get feedback.	**Feedback:** Same as real world when in class, but also think about having students do the task as homework, record it and email it to you as an assessment.	45

© 2007/2008 Languages Out There and its licensors. Reproduction in whole or in part prohibited except as may be provided under the terms of a Licence Agreement. www.languagesoutthere.com

Task Sheet 1

Shopping

1. In pairs, talk about the last time you bought these things:

a DVD	an item of clothing
a piece of jewellery	a present
a book	a sports item

- Where did you buy them?
- How much did they cost?
- Who was the present for?
- What exactly was each item? (describe it in detail)

Vocabulary

2. Where would you do the following?

e.g. I would buy aspirin in a chemist's/pharmacy.

buy a paperback	buy aspirin
borrow a book	change money
buy stamps	buy a CD
buy cosmetics	buy a pair of jeans
have a burger	have a coffee
buy a loaf of bread	have a haircut
log on to the internet	buy some vitamin pills

3. Look at these expressions from a conversation in a clothes shop, and mark them C for customer and A for assistant.

It's OK. I'm just looking.
Have you got these in black?
Can I try these on?
Can I help you?
Would you like to try these on?
Have you got these in a larger size?
How would you like to pay?
What size are you?
These feel a bit tight.
They look a bit tight.
What colour would you like?
Here's your receipt.

Task Sheet 2

Comparatives and superlatives

Your teacher will demonstrate the form, use and examples on the board. Copy them here:

Exercise 1

Work in pairs. You are in a shop. Decide what to say and have a conversation using the words below.

Shop assistant	Customer
Greet the customer.	You want to buy a top and a pair of trousers. Here are the details:
Ask them what they want.	
Ask about size and colour for each item.	top
Ask if the customer wants to try the items on.	size: medium
Give them the price.	colour: light blue
Ask them how they want to pay.	trousers
Offer them a receipt.	size: medium
Say goodbye.	colour: black
	You want to try them on.
	You need a receipt.
	You want to pay by credit card.

Exercise 2

Now change the details of the conversation (item, size, colour, price) and change roles. Make notes below.

Now act out your role-play to the class.

© 2007/2008 Languages Out There and its licensors. Reproduction in whole or in part prohibited except as may be provided under the terms of a Licence Agreement. www.languagesoutthere.com

Out There Task

Real World: In the department store find eight items you would like to buy and describe them here. Include price, size and other features like material. Compare them to other similar items.

VoIP: Visit a website like www.debenhams.co.uk or www.johnlewis.co.uk, find eight items you would like to buy and write descriptions of them. Include price, size and other features like material. Compare them to other similar items:

VoIP: Tell your conversation partners about what you found. Ask them to compare them to their recent or similar purchases.

Lesson Plan

Level 4	Topic	Aim	Language Focus	Skills
Lesson 6	The past of a town or city	To talk about the past	Past simple passive	Reading, speaking, listening

Out There – real world	Out There – VoIP
Take students to a place where people are hanging out and not in a rush. They are generally more approachable if they are sitting down. Think parks, squares and civic spaces where people take a break from their busy day.	Tell students to call conversation partners on VoIP using the school's computers or at home.

#	Details	Task Sheet	Minutes
1	To introduce the theme of the lesson, ask the students what they know about the history of the town or city they are living in/studying in. Elicit as much information as possible and make notes on the board. Encourage them to use the past tense.		10
2	Ask the students to read the statements on Task Sheet 1. Ask them to work in pairs, discuss the statements and decide whether they are true or false. Listen to their answers but <u>don't correct</u> them at this stage.	1	15
3	Now give them Task Sheet 2 and ask them to check their answers in the text. Find out if they were surprised by any of the answers. Tell the students to read again and check vocabulary.	2	20
4	Focus on the use of the past simple passive in the text. Ask the students to underline some examples. Then ask them to look at Task Sheet 3. Tell them to work in pairs and complete the two exercises. Check the answers.	3	20
5	Now go to the *Out There* task. Ask the students to give you the complete forms of the questions they will ask using the prompt words. Check that these are accurate and drill for pronunciation, stress and intonation.		15

Out There Tasks

6	**Real world:** Students ask members of the public their questions to start conversations.	**VoIP:** Students ask conversation partners their questions to start conversations.	40
7	**Feedback:** Ask how it went. Check the students have completed the task. Ask them to list their favourite new expressions and words of the day. Ask if they feel confident with the language taught and get feedback.	**Feedback:** Same as real world when in class, but also think about having students do the task as homework, record it and email it to you as an assessment.	45

© 2007/2008 Languages Out There and its licensors. Reproduction in whole or in part prohibited except as may be provided under the terms of a Licence Agreement. www.languagesoutthere.com

Task Sheet 1

What do you know about London?

Are these statements true or false?

1. London was founded by Julius Caesar

2. The Tower of London was built in the 15th century

3. London was destroyed by an enormous fire in 1666

4. During the 19th century London was the largest city in the world

5. The London Underground was the world's first underground railway system

6. London was the first city in the world to have a population of 1 million

7. More than 300,000 Londoners were killed by bombs in World War II

8. Today London has a population of more than 20 million

9. London has five commercial airports

10. Heathrow is the busiest airport in the world

Now check your answers in the text on Task Sheet 2.

Task Sheet 2

A brief history of London

London was founded by the Romans in AD 43, following the Roman invasion of Britain by Julius Caesar in 55BC. The Romans called this settlement Londinium and this is widely believed to be the origin of the present-day name, although it could also be of Celtic origin. In AD100 London became the capital of Roman Britain and, during the 2nd century AD, had a population of about 60,000. As the Roman Empire declined, however, so did London and by the 5th century AD it was largely abandoned.

By 600 AD the Anglo-Saxons had arrived in Britain, and they built a new settlement near the old Roman city, in the area that is now known as Covent Garden. The next invaders were the Vikings, who attacked the city in 851AD. They burnt the Anglo-Saxon city down and occupied the area for some years until the English King Alfred the Great established peace and moved the city back inside the old Roman defensive walls. This city was known as Ealdwic (meaning Old City) and the name survives to this day in the area of London called Aldwych.

Following his victory at the Battle of Hastings, William the Conqueror was crowned King of England in the newly finished Westminster Abbey on Christmas Day 1066. William granted the citizens of London special privileges, while building a castle in the south east corner of the city to keep them under control. This castle was expanded by later kings and is now known as the Tower of London. It began life as a royal residence but was later used as a prison.

In 1097 William II built Westminster Hall very near Westminster Abbey. The hall was the centrepiece of a new Palace of Westminster, which was the main royal residence throughout the Middle Ages. Westminster became the seat of the royal court and government (and still is today), while its neighbour, the City of London, was a centre of trade and commerce. Eventually, the two neighbouring cities grew together and formed the basis of the centre of modern-day London. In the 12th century London became the capital city of England.

Plague caused enormous problems for Europe in the early 17th century and London was no exception. The plague reached its peak in the Great Plague of 1665-1666. This was the last major outbreak in Europe, possibly due to the disastrous fire that destroyed London in 1666. The Great Fire of London started in Pudding Lane in the City and quickly swept through London's wooden buildings and a large part of the city was destroyed. Rebuilding took more than ten years.

London continued to grow during the 17th century and became the world's largest city from about 1831 to 1925. This growth was aided from 1836 by London's first railways, which put country towns around London within easy reach of the city. The rail network expanded very rapidly which meant that these towns also grew while London itself expanded into the surrounding fields, merging with neighbouring settlements such as Kensington, Putney and Battersea. Traffic congestion on the city's roads led to the construction of the world's first underground railway system in 1863 and this brought further expansion and urbanisation. Soon London became one of the first cities in human history to reach a population of one million, and was the first city with a population of five million.

More than 30,000 Londoners were killed by bombs during World War II and large areas of the city were completely destroyed. The city was rebuilt after the war in a number of architectural styles and this helped to give London the character it has today. In the decades following World War II, large-scale immigration around the world transformed London into one of the most racially and culturally diverse cities in Europe if not the world.

Today London is a thriving cosmopolitan city with a population of 8.5 million (12 million in the metropolitan area). It is also an important transport centre with five commercial airports (including Heathrow, the busiest international airport in the world) and the high-speed rail link to Paris and Brussels via the Channel Tunnel. London is also widely regarded as the world's leading financial centre.

Task Sheet 3

Language Focus: past simple passive

Exercise 1

Rearrange these words to make sentences about London:

1. the was by Romans founded London
2. down Vikings the London burnt by was
3. in William crowned 1066 king was
4. prison of as London the used a was Tower
5. system built world's the 1863 underground first was in
6. Londoners killed bombs WWII were by 30,000 in
7. completely of the were areas destroyed city large
8. war rebuilt the after the was city

Exercise 2

Fill the gaps in the sentences using these verbs in the past simple passive:

cause	burn	grant	occupy	bomb	rebuild
		build	use		

1. The original city of London _____ _____ on the north bank of the River Thames by the Romans.
2. London _____ _____ by the Vikings.
3. A large part of London _____ _____ down in the Great Fire.
4. London _____ _____ during World War II.
5. The Tower of London _____ _____ as a prison.
6. The citizens of London _____ _____ special privileges by William the Conqueror.
7. Enormous problems _____ _____ by the 17th century plague.
8. London _____ _____ after the Great Fire.

Out There Task

Real world – To start your conversation, say to people: 'Excuse me, I am learning English. Can I ask you some questions please?' If you work in pairs one person should speak while the other writes. Swap roles for the next person you speak to. Talk to at least four people each about their city.

VoIP – Call conversation partners and ask them these questions to start a conversation. Remember you can record your conversation to listen to later. Find out as much as you can about the following aspects of their town/city:

1. its foundation (when, who)

2. political control (who ruled it)

3. wars, conflicts and other problems

4. commercial and transport history

5. any famous people

6. cultural history and cultural life

© 2007/2008 Languages Out There and its licensors. Reproduction in whole or in part prohibited except as may be provided under the terms of a Licence Agreement. www.languagesoutthere.com

TD4 06

Notes

Lesson Plan

Level 4	Topic	Aim	Language Focus	Skills
Lesson 7	Magazines and newspapers	To discuss magazines and reading	Present perfect and vocabulary on magazines and reading	Reading, speaking, listening

Out There – real world	Out There – VoIP
Take the class to a well-populated area of the town or city, somewhere where people are not in a rush and are easy to approach (i.e. sitting down).	Tell students to use VoIP to call conversation partners using the school's computers or at home.

#	Details	Task Sheet	Minutes
1	To introduce the aim and task of the day, bring into class some popular magazines and ask the students if they have ever read any of them. Write full answers on the board, making mistakes in the tense or word order and ask the students if they can correct it, e.g. 'I read never this magazine'. Explain what you are going to work on.		10
2	Ask the students to do the magazine and newspaper survey. Discuss the answers in open class.	1	15
3	Presentation: present perfect. Elicit highlight form in three uses: experience (I have been to Paris), recent change (I have bought a new car) and continuing situation (I have worked here for four years). Elicit for/since. Past simple: completed action with past time expressions. Now ask the students to do the practice exercise. Check the answers.	2	20
4	Ask the students to look at Task Sheet 3, read the article about *Cosmopolitan* magazine and answer the questions. Ask them to compare their answers with a partner and then check the answers in open class.	3	15
5	Give details of the *Out There* task: ask the students to make two more questions to ask the people. Help and make sure the questions are about the topic of the day. Check pronunciation and intonation and discuss possible answers.		10

Out There Tasks

#	Real world / VoIP		Minutes
6	**Real world:** Students ask members of the public their questions to start conversations.	**VoIP:** Students ask conversation partners their questions to start conversations.	40
7	**Feedback:** Ask how it went. Check the students have completed the task. Ask them to list their favourite new expressions and words of the day. Ask if they feel confident with the language taught and get feedback.	**Feedback:** Same as real world when in class, but also think about having students do the task as homework, record it and email it to you as an assessment.	45

© 2007/2008 Languages Out There and its licensors. Reproduction in whole or in part prohibited except as may be provided under the terms of a Licence Agreement. www.languagesoutthere.com

Task Sheet 1

Reading habits: present perfect vs past simple.

What's your favourite newspaper and/or magazine, and why? Discuss with a partner.

Find out more about people's attitudes to newspapers and magazines. Complete this survey and then discuss your answers.

Newspaper and magazine questionnaire.

Have you heard of these newspapers and magazines?

Newspapers/magazines:	Have you heard of it?	Have you ever read it?	When did you last read it?
The Times			
New York Times			
International Herald Tribune			
Le Monde			
The Sun			
El Pais			
Hello!			
Time			
Der Spiegel			
FHM			
Cosmopolitan			
Paris Match			
Big Issue			

Have you read any other newspapers or magazines this week? If so, which ones?

Where do you read newspapers or magazines? Complete this table:

	usually	sometimes	never
at home			
waiting for the doctor or dentist			
in newsagents shops or at newsstands in the street			
at work or school			
in bed			
on the train			
on the plane			
on holiday			
other places or situations			

© 2007/2008 Languages Out There and its licensors. Reproduction in whole or in part prohibited except as may be provided under the terms of a Licence Agreement. www.languagesoutthere.com

Task Sheet 2

Present perfect

Form: *For/ Since
  *
  *
  *
  *

Uses:

1.

2.

3.

Timeline

Past Simple

Use

Write true sentences about yourself containing these time expressions and using the past simple or present perfect simple:

#	Sentence	Time expression
1	_____	last Sunday
2	_____	since 2001
3	_____	last year
4	_____	two months ago
5	_____	already
6	_____	for the last six months
7	_____	the day before yesterday
8	_____	still
9	_____	all my life
10	_____	when I was young

Task Sheet 3

Cosmopolitan

Read this text about a magazine for women:

Cosmopolitan (often referred to as *Cosmo*) was first published in 1886. It began life as a 'family magazine' with articles on fashion, household decoration, cooking and the care and management of children. In its first year *Cosmopolitan's* circulation reached 25,000. In 1889 a new editor introduced colour illustrations, serials and book reviews. It also became a leading market for fiction, featuring such authors as Rudyard Kipling and Jack London. By 1892 its circulation had reached 75,000.

In the 1930s, *Cosmopolitan* had a circulation of 1.7 million and an advertising income of $5,000,000. In the 1940s it focused on fiction and was subtitled *The Four-Book Magazine* since the first section had one novelette, six or eight short stories, two serials, six to eight articles and eight or nine special features, while the other three sections featured two novels. During World War II, sales reached 2 million. The magazine contained less fiction during the 1950s.

The circulation of *Cosmopolitan* dropped to slightly over a million by 1955, and it continued to fall until the late 1960s when it became a women's magazine. Though *Cosmopolitan* is known for its sex advice and sex tips, the magazine mainly focuses on providing coverage of the latest in fashion and beauty. It regularly contains 'real-life' stories, safety tips for risky or dangerous situations (such as living alone), features on health, celebrity gossip and advice on relationships. *Cosmopolitan* is now the world's biggest-selling women's magazine.

Now answer these questions:

1. Cosmopolitan was first published in _____.

2. It began life as a _____.

3. By 1955 it was selling slightly over a _____ copies a month.

4. During Word War II, its circulation reached _____.

5. In the 1930s its advertising income reached _____.

6. It became a women's magazine in the late _____.

7. It is now the world's _____ women's magazine.

8. In the early years Cosmopolitan focused mainly _____.

Out There Task

Real world – to start your conversation say to people: "Excuse me, I am learning English. Can I ask you some questions please?" If you work in pairs one person should speak while the other writes. Swap roles for the next person you speak to. Talk to at least four people each. Make the last two questions yourself.

VoIP – call conversation partners and ask them these questions to start a conversation. Make the last two questions yourself. Remember you can record your conversation to listen to later.

1. What magazines have you read recently?

2. How often do you read magazines?

3. Where do you usually read magazines?

4.

5.

Notes

Lesson Plan

Level 4	Topic	Aim	Language Focus	Skills
Lesson 8	Diaries/slang/true stories	To enable students to talk and write about past events	Past continuous/past simple	Reading, speaking, writing, listening

Out There – real world	Out There – VoIP
Find a place close to the school where lots of people are sitting down relaxing, like a small park or a square. Tell students not to forget to use the 'magic words' and to smile!	Tell students to call conversation partners using VoIP.

#	Details	Task Sheet	Minutes
1	To introduce the aim and task of the day. Ask if students have a diary. What do they use it for? Different uses, appointments, reminders etc. Check the use of the present continuous for definite arrangements in the future.		10
2	Hand out Task Sheet 1. Ask the students to read the text and ask them to match the meanings of the slang words in bold to the definitions. Then tell them to write a few sentences about themselves using the slang.	1	20
3	Task Sheet 2. Students read the diary entry and match the words to the definitions.	2	15
4	Task Sheet 3: Exercise 1. Students look at the text in Task Sheet 2 again and underline all the past simple and past continuous verbs. Then they complete the rule.	3	10
5	Then ask students to look at Exercise 2. They should fill the gaps using either the past simple or past continuous forms of the verbs in brackets. Check the answers in open class.	3	15
6	Give details of the *Out There* task.		5

	Out There Tasks		
7	**Real world:** Students ask members of the public their questions to start conversations.	**VoIP:** Students ask conversation partners their questions to start conversations.	40
8	**Feedback:** Ask how it went. Check the students have completed the task. Ask them to report back using different past tenses and to list their favourite new expressions and words of the day. Ask if they feel confident with the language taught and get feedback.	**Feedback:** Same as real world when in class, but also think about having students do the task as homework, record it and email it to you as an assessment.	45

© 2007/2008 Languages Out There and its licensors. Reproduction in whole or in part prohibited except as may be provided under the terms of a Licence Agreement. www.languagesoutthere.com

Task Sheet 1

Can you guess the meaning of the slang words in *italics* in the diary entry below?

> **Yesterday's diary:**
>
> Went to London today. There was a ***bloke*** on the train talking to himself. He looked a bit of a ***nutter*** so I didn't sit next to him. Don't like ***dodgy-looking*** people like that. It was warm in the train and I couldn't keep my eyes open. Felt a bit ***knackered*** after getting up so early. After a while I ***dropped*** off. Must have had a good ***kip*** because when I woke up we were nearly in London. Noticed that the strange-looking ***bloke*** was sitting opposite me. He was still talking to himself. Asked me for a ***fag.*** Said he didn't have any ***dosh*** to buy any himself. Felt a bit sorry for the ***bloke*** so I gave him 50p. I'm always doing ***daft*** things like that. Went to a cafe at Victoria station and found a £10 note on the floor. I was really ***chuffed.*** I'd just made a profit of £9.50.

Match the highlighted words with these definitions:

1. strange-looking
2. tired
3. cigarette
4. money
5. pleased with myself
6. man
7. crazy person
8. stupid
9. fell asleep
10. sleep

Write a few sentences about yourself using some of the slang words from the text:

-
-
-
-

Task Sheet 2

A personal story

Read the text of a personal journal entry and match the highlighted words and phrases from the text with a meaning:

Journal entry, May 28th 2007

The strangest thing happened to me last Friday. I was walking down the road to the supermarket to buy a disposable barbecue and I saw a woman with two **kids**. I thought they looked familiar but didn't think twice about it. As I was passing her she said, "Hi Pete!" I turned around and who did I see, an old **mate** from **way back** in New Zealand. We embraced and **caught up** on a lot as I hadn't seen her for at least five years. We'd lost each other's contact details and didn't **have a clue** where in the world the other was. **On top of that**, a mutual friend of ours was coming to visit this weekend. The three of us were best friends when we were studying back in New Zealand in **the late 80's**. They also didn't know of each other's whereabouts or how to contact each other. The three of us **hung out** together and we had a great weekend. But **to top it all off**, I discovered that she has just moved here with her new family and of all the places in London, she only lives ten minutes' walk from my house. Now that's incredible!

1. kids
2. mate
3. way back
4. caught up
5. on top of that
6. the late 80's
7. hung out
8. to top it all off
9. didn't have a clue

a. in addition
b. **1.** and the worst thing is; **2.** and the best thing is.
c. children
d. spent time together
e. a long time ago
f. didn't know
g. told each other about our lives
h. friend
i. 1986-1989

Task Sheet 3

Exercise 1

Read the text again. Underline all the past simple verbs and then do the same with the past continuous verbs.

Past continuous vs past simple.

Look at the following statement and choose the correct ending:

We use past simple and past continuous together when ...

a. a shorter action happened during a longer action.
b. one action happened before another action.
c. an action started in the past and hasn't finished yet.

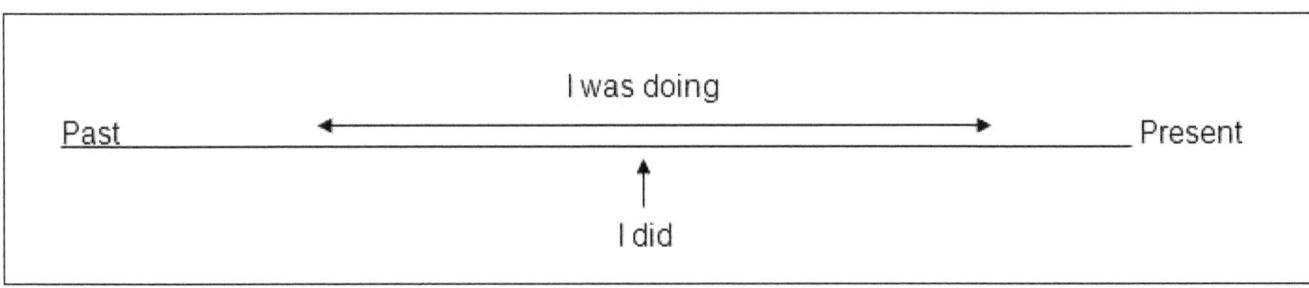

Exercise 2

Look at the following sentences and fill in the gaps with the correct form of the verb in brackets. Use only past simple or past continuous. The first one has been done for you:

1. While he _____ (play) football it _____ (start) to rain.
   While he was playing football it started to rain.

2. While I _____ (drop off) the kids ___ at school I ____ (see) an old mate and we _____ (catch up) over a coffee.

3. I ____ (get) married way back in the late 70's when I _____ (study) at Oxford university.

4. My friend's handbag _____ (be stolen) while she _____ (wait) for the train, and to top it all off she _____ (sprain) her ankle.

5. I _____ (not go) to the cinema because I _____ (hang out) with my parents.

6. While I _____ (drive) down Regent Street, someone _____ (ask) me where Oxford street was. I _____ (not have) a clue because I _____ (be) new to London.

Out There Task

Real world – To start your conversation, say to people: 'Excuse me, I am learning English. Can I ask you some questions please?' If you work in pairs, one should speak while the other writes. Swap roles for the next person you speak to. Talk to at least four people each.

VoIP – Call conversation partners and ask them these questions to start a conversation. Remember you can record your conversation to listen to later.

Ask people to tell you about an interesting experience that happened to them in the past. Listen, in particular, for their use of the past tense. Use the following headings to take notes:

When did it happen?

Where did it happen?

Who was involved?

What were they doing?

What did you do?

Now tell your conversation partners about your past experiences using different past tenses.

© 2007/2008 Languages Out There and its licensors. Reproduction in whole or in part prohibited except as may be provided under the terms of a Licence Agreement. www.languagesoutthere.com

TD4 08

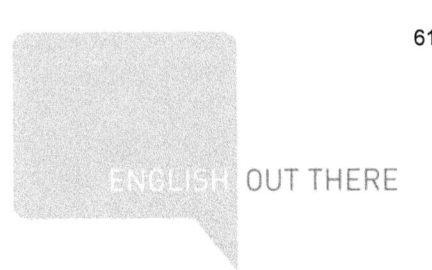

Notes

Lesson Plan

Level 4	Topic	Aim	Language Focus	Skills
Lesson 9	Travel advice	To get travel and tourist advice	Expressing degrees of obligation and advice - modals	Speaking, reading, listening

Out There – real world	*Out There* – VoIP
Find a place close to the school where lots of people are sitting down relaxing, like a small park or a square. Tell students not to forget to use the 'magic words' and to smile	Tell students to use VoIP to call conversation partners on the school's computers or at home.

#	Details	Task Sheet	Minutes
1	To introduce the aim and task of the day, write on the board: 'You should eat seafood which isn't fresh' – ask students to say if this is good advice. Elicit the correct form (mustn't) and explain that in this lesson you are going to learn about obligation and advice.		5
2	Encourage the students to think of the best holiday they ever had - where, when, who with.		5
3	Task Sheet 1: ask the students to do the matching activity. Do one example on the board first. Then check the answers and focus on the differences in meaning. Key: 1. c; 2. a;,3. d;,4. e; 5. b; 6. f; then a. 2; b. 4; c. 5; d. 3; e. 1; f. 6.	1	30
4	Task Sheet 2: use the advertisements for tourist destinations and/or holidays to provide vocabulary (add some real ones if you can). Tell students to write sentences about each location.	2	20
5	To practise the vocabulary, and get the students thinking about what people usually do on holidays, ask them to complete the postcard. Include vocabulary for sightseeing, shopping, accommodation, food, entertainment, photographs and spending.	3	10
6	Explain the *Out There* task. Students write questions to ask people.		10
H/W	For homework you can ask the students to right a similar leaflet with tips and advice for British tourists visiting their country.		

Out There Tasks			
7	**Real world:** Students work in pairs asking members of the public their questions to start conversations. One writes while one speaks. Then swap.	**VoIP:** Students ask conversation partners their questions to start conversations.	40
8	**Feedback:** Ask how it went. Check the students have completed the task. Ask them to list their favourite new expressions and words of the day. Ask if they feel confident with the language taught and get feedback.	**Feedback:** Same as real world when in class, but also think about having students do the task as homework, record it and email it to you as an assessment.	45

© 2007/2008 Languages Out There and its licensors. Reproduction in whole or in part prohibited except as may be provided under the terms of a Licence Agreement. www.languagesoutthere.com

Task Sheet 1

Modals of advice and obligation

1. Match these sentence beginnings with the most suitable endings:

   1. You have to/must
   2. You should
   3. You don't have to
   4. You shouldn't
   5. You mustn't
   6. You'd better

   A. send a postcard to your family
   B. eat seafood which isn't fresh
   C. pay for a meal in a restaurant
   D. take sun cream, when you visit London
   E. take a lot of cash
   F. not forget your keys, otherwise you'll be in trouble

2. Compare your answers with a partner and then decide which of these explanations best describes one of the completed sentences above:

   A. It's a good idea to do it.

   B. It isn't a good idea to do it.

   C. Strong advice.

   D. You can do it if you want but it's not necessary.

   E. It's necessary or an obligation to do this.

   F. It's wrong or dangerous or sometimes not permitted.

3. Study these sentences and decide if they are logical or not. If they aren't logical, correct them:

Example: You have to put lemon in tea or coffee.
Answer: Not logical. You don't have to put anything in tea or coffee, but you can if you want.

   You have to drink wine if you are taking medicine.

   You shouldn't have travel insurance.

   You don't have to tell the police when you arrive in a new country.

   You should arrive at the airport two hours before the plane leaves.

   You mustn't forget your passport if you leave the country.

   You don't have to take photographs.

   You mustn't book a hotel room before you go on holidays.

   You don't have to drink a lot of water if you are in the sun.

Task Sheet 2

Holiday in England

Read these advertisements for six different holidays in England:

London! Spend two weeks in exciting London. Theatre, dance, shopping, museums and pubs... everything is here for you to enjoy. Amazing!

Kent! The Garden of England - Canterbury and the Kent coast are rich in history, with outstanding scenery and attractions and events to keep you entertained.

Do it yourself! We provide the car or van, maps and advice, and you go your own way discovering the England you want to discover.

The South East! All along the coast there is windsurfing, sailing and canoeing. In the countryside, hire a mountain bike and go on rough terrain, or why not go horse riding.

Dover! White cliff country. The landscape is unforgettable and the views from the cliffs of Dover are simply breathtaking. A wonderful place to visit for you, your family and friends.

Colchester! Britain's oldest recorded town. For a great day out, visit a place with history, art and fantastic places to relax.

What can we imagine about these holidays? Write some sentences about a few locations.
(Use should/ shouldn't/ must/ mustn't/ have to/ don't have to).

For example: 'If you go to Colchester you don't have to take lots of money' or 'If you go to Colchester you don't have to do anything at all if you want to rest'.

Task Sheet 3

Complete this postcard that Andy sent to his family while he was on holiday. You may need a word or phrase in each space:

Hi everyone, I've been in Prague for three days now and I'm having a (1)_____ time. I spent the first day (2)_____. I saw the Old Town, the Charles Bridge, Prague Castle and Wenceslas Square. A lot of the historic part of Prague is (3)_____ of tourists especially at this time of year. So yesterday I decided to (4)_____ a trip to the countryside. I (5)_____ by train to a little village called Karlstejn, about 30 kilometres south-west of Prague. There's an amazing castle there which (6)_____ like something out of a Dracula movie. I (7)_____ lunch in a little restaurant just below the castle. The food was fantastic and so was the beer. Everything is so (8)_____ here. The meal cost (9)_____ than three pounds! This morning I (10)_____ a bit of shopping and (11)_____ some presents for you all. See you soon!

All the best, Andy

Out There Task

Real world - To start a conversation, say to people: 'Excuse me, I am learning English. Can I ask you some questions please?'

VoIP – Call your conversation partners and ask them these questions to start a conversation. Remember you can record your conversation to listen to later.

Think about the following topics and get information, examples and prices. Then add some of your own.

Before you ask your questions, remember to explain that you are looking for travel advice and wish to practise your English.

Topic	Your questions	Your answers
Food and drink		
Where to go, e.g. sightseeing		
Places to stay, e.g. hotels		
When to go (time of year)		
Travel and tickets		
What to take		
Entertainment		
People and culture		
Other		

Notes

Lesson Plan

Level 4	Topic	Aim	Language Focus	Skills
Lesson 10	Beauty	To assess whether ideas of beauty are cross-cultural	Adjectives	Reading speaking, listening

Out There – real world	*Out There* – VoIP
Visit an art gallery or take the class to a well-populated area of the town or city, somewhere where people are not in a rush and are easy to approach (i.e. sitting down).	Tell students to use VoIP to call some conversation partners.

#	Details	Task Sheet	Minutes
1	To introduce the aim and task of the day show the class the picture of *African Beauty* and ask the questions leading to 'what do you consider beautiful?' Write the answers on the board. If there are any mistakes, ask the class to correct them and explain the focus of the lesson.	1	5
2	Adjectives game - ask the students to work in pairs and list as many adjectives as they can to describe how someone looks e.g. attractive, pretty, handsome etc.	2	10
3	Give students pictures from magazines and ask them to compile lists of what is considered to be beautiful physically in both men and women – are these ideas the same in different cultures?		10
4	Ask the students to work in pairs and discuss the questions in Exercise 2 on appearance. Listen to their ideas. Then ask them to work in small groups and discuss the questions in Exercise 3.	2	20
5	Give the students Task Sheet 3. Ask them to find the answers to the questions in the text by scan reading.	3	10
6	Ask the students to read the text. Then ask them if they agree with the different concepts of beauty.	3	15
7	Explain the *Out There* task. (students add two more questions for speaking task.)	4	10

	Out There Tasks		
8	**Real world:** Students describe art that is beautiful. Or ask members of the public their questions to start conversations.	**VoIP:** Students ask conversation partners their questions to start conversations.	40
9	**Feedback:** Ask how it went. Check the students have completed the task. Ask them to list their favourite new expressions and words of the day. Ask if they feel confident with the language taught and get feedback.	**Feedback:** Same as real world when in class, but also think about having students do the task as homework, record it and email it to you as an assessment.	45

© 2007/2008 Languages Out There and its licensors. Reproduction in whole or in part prohibited except as may be provided under the terms of a Licence Agreement. www.languagesoutthere.com

Task Sheet 1

http://www.lammart.lu/African_Beauty.jpg

This is called *African Beauty*.

Do you think it's beautiful?

Why? Why not?

What do you consider beautiful?

Task Sheet 2

Exercise 1: Adjectives

In pairs list as many adjectives as you can to describe how someone looks e.g. attractive, pretty, handsome etc.

Divide the adjectives into three groups: positive, negative and neutral.

Exercise 2: Appearance

Talk about these questions with a partner:

1. How often do you look in the mirror each day?
2. Do you worry about your appearance?
3. Do you sometimes put clothes on and then take them off and try something different?
4. Do people look better with or without make-up?
5. Do you think people look better with a suntan?
6. What is more important – appearance or personality?

Compare your ideas with the group.

Exercise 3: Discussion

Discuss these questions in small groups:

1. Is physical attractiveness more important in men or women?
2. Do most people worry too much about their appearance?
3. Does someone's physical appearance influence their personality?
4. Is beauty only physical?
5. Do you agree with cosmetic surgery?
6. Do 'good-looking' people have more success in their careers?
7. 'Beauty is in the eye of the beholder.'

Task Sheet 3

Answer these questions from the article on human beauty:

- Why does attractiveness matter?

- How has evolution been affected by beauty?

- What problems do very attractive women have?

What is human beauty?

The way people look is more important than we might think. The genetic make-up our ancestors have given us through their genes matters a great deal. Beauty plays a crucial role in people's lives. It may not be politically correct to say that appearance matters and many people believe that that it should not matter. But that is surely an idealistic view. It is quite clear that in many walks of life people's relative attractiveness influences what other people think of them.

There appear to be a number of clear advantages to being attractive. First of all, attractive people tend to find attractive partners. Secondly, teachers and other people who give grades and marks (such as driving test examiners) often give better grades to attractive people because they see them as being more intelligent and sociable than less attractive-looking people. Thirdly, a number of studies have shown that attractive people are treated more leniently in court when they face criminal charges.

The main biological purpose of beauty is to attract the attention of the opposite sex and the main biological purpose of sex is reproduction. This is true of both the animal world and the human world. Our brains and minds have been shaped by evolution in such a way that faces and bodies that seem the most suitable for healthy reproduction are the ones that we find the most attractive and, indeed, beautiful. Women tend to find tall men more attractive than short men. This is because tallness equates with power and status and therefore suggests to women that such men might be able to provide them with the resources they will need to raise a family.

Almost everyone finds babies beautiful and cute. We also tend to find beautiful babies even more beautiful. Research has shown that beautiful babies get more attention from their mothers. They talk to them more and look into their eyes more than the mothers of less attractive babies do. It appears that the mothers of attractive babies devote more energy to fulfilling physical needs such as feeding. This probably has its basis deep in the mists of time when mothers devoted more time and energy to healthier-looking babies because these had more chance of survival than weaker, ill or unattractive babies.

Different cultures seem to have different ideas about what is considered attractive. Often the most beautiful face is that which is typical of a particular culture or environment. It seems that we find typical faces attractive because they suggest something that has adapted to a particular environment. Typical faces may also suggest that their owners are healthy people. As the world becomes more cosmopolitan in this age of globalisation, however, it is quite possible that our ideas of what is typical and therefore beautiful may also change and develop.

There are two sides to human beauty. It may not always be a positive thing. For example, some beautiful teenage girls may find it difficult to form strong friendships and relationships with other girls and with boys. They may have problems with women because other females may be jealous of them because they think they will take their men away. Very attractive women often have trouble keeping their female friends as a result. At the same time they might think that men simply want them because of their attractive appearance and are not interested in their minds or their feelings.

Which parts of the text do you agree with? Discuss with your partner.

Out There Task

Real world - Approach people and say: 'Excuse me, I am learning English. Can I ask you some questions please?'

VoIP – Call conversation partners and ask them these questions to start a conversation. Remember you can record your conversation to listen to later.

Ask people these questions:

Why do you think people worry about their appearance?

Is physical attractiveness more important in men or women? Why?

What do you consider to be beautiful?

What do you think about cosmetic surgery?

Out There Task

Today we will be looking at works of art from different cultures and artists. Choose at least four and describe the people in them using adjectives from the class. Think about these questions:

Do you find them beautiful, ugly or scary etc.?

Why?

Lesson Plan

Level 4	Topic	Aim	Language Focus	Skills
Lesson 11	Lies	To enable students to make admissions and apologise	Should have + past participle, I wish I had + past participle. Formal/informal	Reading, speaking, listening

Out There – real world	*Out There* – VoIP
Find a place close to the school where lots of people are sitting down relaxing, like a small park or a square. Tell students not to forget to use the 'magic words' and to smile!	Tell students to use VoIP to call some conversation partners.

#	Details	Task Sheet	Minutes
1	To introduce the aim and task of the day, tell the class a short story about someone you know who went to a job interview and didn't get the job because they were drunk. Ask the students to make a sentence about this using shouldn't. ('He shouldn't have been drunk') and if they don't get it right, introduce shouldn't have + past participle.		10
2	Show the class some pictures of people that are inappropriately dressed or behaving inappropriately during interviews (use some magazine pictures for this purpose). Explain that the people in the pictures didn't get the jobs and encourage the students to say why (e.g. 'She shouldn't have worn so much jewellery/He should have worn a suit etc').		20
3	Task Sheet 1: ask the students to read the text and put the paragraphs in the correct order. Then ask them to work in pairs and say what Jack and the interviewer should and shouldn't have done using complete sentences.	1	20
4	Task Sheet 2: ask the students to decide which conversation these sentences come from.	2	10
5	Task Sheet 3: ask the students to work in pairs, choose a role-play and act out the conversation. Act out the role-plays in class.	3	15
6	Give details of the *Out There* task.		5

Out There Tasks		
7	**Real world:** Students ask members of the public their questions to start conversations.	**VoIP:** Students ask conversation partners their questions to start conversations.	40
8	**Feedback:** Ask how it went. Check the students have completed the task. Ask them to list their favourite new expressions and words of the day. Ask if they feel confident with the language taught and get feedback,	**Feedback:** Same as real world when in class, but also think about having students do the task as homework, record it and email it to you as an assessment.	45

© 2007/2008 Languages Out There and its licensors. Reproduction in whole or in part prohibited except as may be provided under the terms of a Licence Agreement. www.languagesoutthere.com

Task Sheet 1

Can you drive?

A: "It's no good. They'll never accept me. They want people who can drive and I haven't got a licence".
Phil laughed. "That's not a problem. Just tell them you've got a licence. They're not going to ask to see it, are they?" Jack thought for a moment and then he picked up the telephone …

B: "Well, that seems to be all," said Mr Hodges, the man who was interviewing Jack. "Oh, just a moment. There is one more thing. Can I just check that you've got a driving licence? You probably won't need to do any driving but from time to time our people have to visit other places for work and some of them don't have rail services." Jack hesitated for a moment and then said "Er… yes, yes I do. I've got a full driving licence. I passed my test five years ago".

C: Jack had been doing the same boring job for more than three years. Every day he sat at his computer and typed lists of figures. Pages and pages, hour after hour, day after day. On this particular day he was really bored. He stared at the wall. "I should have paid more attention when I was at school," he thought. "And I should have gone to university to get some proper qualifications. I might be able to get a better job then". He carried on typing.

D: It was three months later and Jack had already been at his new job in Edinburgh for six weeks when the telephone rang. It was Mr Hodges. "Hello, Jack. How are things? Listen we need you to go on a business trip tomorrow. There's no train service so you'll have to take the company car. I'll bring the keys over this afternoon and give you the details." Jack went pale…

E: Then Jack's colleague Phil came over to the desk. He was holding a newspaper. "Have you seen this?" he said. "They're looking for computer-literate people to work for a new company in Edinburgh. No experience needed and £600 a week. That's £250 more than we're getting here. Look!" Jack took the newspaper and read the advertisement carefully. Yes, it was true. The money was good and the job sounded easy. There was a problem though. Applicants had to have a driving licence. Jack couldn't drive.

Put the parts of the text in the right order:

1. _____ 2. _____ 3. _____ 4. _____ 5. _____

Work with a partner. Write down at least three things that you believe Jack or the interviewer should or shouldn't have done. Use complete sentences:

Task Sheet 2

Formal or informal?

Look at these expressions and decide which conversation they belong to:

1. Jack and Phil (informal)
2. Jack and Mr Hodges (formal)

Put (1) if you think it belongs to the first conversation, (2) for the second or (?) if it could be in either conversation.

1. What's up? You look a bit worried.
2. There are several issues we need to discuss.
3. I should never have listened to you.
4. I wish I'd never seen that ad in the first place.
5. There's something important I need to speak to you about.
6. I think you'd better tell him the truth. It'd be much easier in the long run.
7. I'm afraid there's been a slight misunderstanding.
8. Oh, for heaven's sake. Just tell him!
9. I'm afraid this is a very serious matter.
10. Why on earth did you think you could get away with it.
11. You should have been honest with me at the interview.
12. You should have taken some driving lessons and passed your test.
13. Are you OK? Is something wrong?
14. Well, what do you expect? You lied, didn't you?
15. Is everything alright, Jack? You seem a bit quiet today.
16. I'm afraid there's something I need to tell you.
17. You leave me with very little option.
18. I'm afraid we take this sort of thing rather seriously.

Task Sheet 3

Roleplay

Work with a partner. Read the text again if necessary. Then choose one of the roleplays and practise the possible conversation together:

Roleplay 1:   A. You are Phil. Jack is very worried about something. Try to find out what it is. Ask questions:

- what's the matter?
- what happened...?
- what are you going to...?

Give Jack some advice.

B. You are Jack. Tell Phil about your problem. When you have told him, listen to his advice, and accept or reject it.

Roleplay 2:   A. You are Mr Hodges. Jack has been working for you for six weeks now and now you want him to drive down to the Borders (the area between Scotland and England) to visit an important client.

B. You are Jack. You can't drive so you either have to think of an excuse or admit the truth.

Now act out your conversation for another pair and listen to their role-play. Are they similar? What are the differences?

Discussion:

1. Is it ever acceptable to lie?
2. What do you think Jack should do?
3. What should/shouldn't he have done?

Out There Task

Real world - say: 'Excuse me, I'm learning English. Can I ask you a few questions please?' Then ask people these questions while your partner writes the answers. Swap roles for the next person.

VoIP - Call conversation partners and ask them these questions to start a conversation. Remember you can record your conversation to listen to later.

Questions	1st Person	2nd Person	3rd Person	4th Person	5th Person
What is inappropriate at a job interview?					
What lies are told in job interviews?					
Do you feel these lies are justified?					
In general, what sorts of lies do you think are justified? Can you give me some examples?					
Can you think of a lie a friend told you, which you couldn't forgive them for?					
Or a lie you told someone, which they couldn't forgive you for?					

© 2007/2008 Languages Out There and its licensors. Reproduction in whole or in part prohibited except as may be provided under the terms of a Licence Agreement. www.languagesoutthere.com

TD4 11

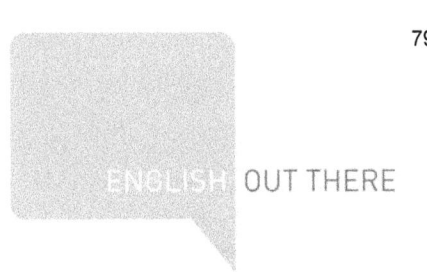

Notes

Lesson Plan

Level 4	Topic	Aim	Language Focus	Skills
Lesson 12	Jobs	To enable students to find out information about jobs	Vocabulary on jobs and skills	Reading, speaking, listening

Out There – real world	Out There – VoIP
Find a place close to the school where lots of people are sitting down relaxing, like a small park or a square. Tell students not to forget to use the 'magic words' and to smile!	Tell students to call conversation partners using VoIP.

#	Details	Task Sheet	Minutes
1	To introduce the aim of the lesson, tell the class that your friend wants to work as a fitness instructor (for example). Ask the students to suggest what they think this job requires and try to elicit qualifications, skills, personality and any other related points. Explain the task and the aim of this lesson.		5
2	Task Sheet 1: ask the students to work in pairs to discuss the differences between the two words and then list some unusual jobs. Discuss some unusual jobs in open class. Focus attention on the pre-reading questions in Exercise 2. Check understanding.	1	15
3	Hand out Task Sheet 2 (job adverts) and allow five minutes for students to find answers to the questions. Go through new vocabulary and pronunciation. Check in pairs and as a group.	2	10
4	Tell the students to do Exercises 1 and 2 to build vocabulary. Check answers in open class.	3	20
5	Describing jobs: use the students' jobs if possible as examples and prepare descriptions. Allow time for students to write them and then swap with partners and discuss similarities, the best/worst paid, skills etc. Encourage use of the new vocabulary, monitor and help with pronunciation.		20
6	Explain the *Out There* task. Using the jobs they have found online, students interview at least four people and find out if they are interested in the jobs. Explore the reasons why/why not.		10

	Out There Tasks		
7	**Real world:** Students ask members of the public their questions to start conversations.	**VoIP:** Students find jobs online and then ask conversation partners which they would or wouldn't like.	40
8	**Feedback:** Ask how it went. Check the students have completed the task. Ask them to list their favourite new expressions and words of the day. Ask if they feel confident with the language taught and get feedback	**Feedback:** Same as real world when in class, but also think about having students do the task as homework, record it and email it to you as an assessment.	45

© 2007/2008 Languages Out There and its licensors. Reproduction in whole or in part prohibited except as may be provided under the terms of a Licence Agreement. www.languagesoutthere.com

Task Sheet 1

Jobs and work

Exercise 1

What is the difference between a *job* and *work*? Give some examples.

Make a list of the most unusual jobs you've ever come across:

Exercise 2

Read the three job advertisements on the next page and answer the following questions:

- Which job is part-time?

- Which job is the best paid?

- Which job requires language skills?

- Which job requires a qualification in computing?

- Which job doesn't offer a salary?

- Which job requires a team leader?

- Which one would you apply for?

Task Sheet 2

1. Head Chef

Organisation: LAZAT **Location:** Essex
Salary: Salary up to £17,500 according to experience.

Job description
Head Chef required minimum 3 years experience as a chef for an expanding and busy restaurant, for daily management of the kitchen staff, food presentation, stock control and service. English/Urdu essential.

Adapted from: http://jobs.guardian.co.uk/browse/catering/general/vacancy-w49777.html

2.
Head of Computer Services
Organisation: Rethink Recruitment
Location: Cambridgeshire
Salary: £50,364

WHEN IT COMES TO THE LATEST TECHNOLOGY
WE'RE ALWAYS FIRST ON THE SCENE

With a job as vital as ours, it will come as no surprise that we need the latest technology to stay one step ahead. We're currently seeking talented IT professionals to join us at an exciting time of change. And not only will you benefit from working with cutting edge technology, you'll also enjoy a genuine work/life balance, excellent training and all the benefits of working in one of the UK's most beautiful, and well connected areas.

Heading a team of 30 IT staff, covering all aspects of development and technical project delivery you will have 5-7 years' experience in computing and technical project management and experience of managing a comparable IT department. A degree or equivalent in computing is essential.

The role requires a full driving licence.

ReThink Recruitment

- CAMBRIDGESHIRE CONSTABULARY -
Creating a safer Cambridgeshire

http://jobs.guardian.co.uk/browse/it-and-telecoms/development/vacancy-1124242-6.html

3. Trustee Voluntary Post – Communications
Organisation: WOODLAND TRUST
Location: Lincolnshire
Salary: Voluntary Post

Job description
We are looking to recruit a Trustee with relevant skills and experience in communications to join our Council of Trustees during 2006.

Technical knowledge, the ability to work as part of a team, the ability to distinguish between the Council's governance role and the staff's management role are key attributes, and it is helpful if Council can reflect a diverse range of perspectives from a cross-section of society.

You will be committed to the Trust and its values, able to act without regard to your personal interests, be assertive yet collaborative, willing to devote a reasonable amount of time and energy, have a high level of integrity, and understand and accept the legal duties and responsibilities of being a Trustee and a Director. But, above all, you will have a passion for woodland, the environment and effective communications.

The role involves around 12 days pa, of which about half relates to Council meetings, but initially there will also be a tailored induction programme. Reasonable expenses will be reimbursed.

http://jobs.guardian.co.uk/browse/volunteers/environmental/vacancy-w47746.html

Task Sheet 3

Exercise 1

Look at the job adverts and find words for each of these categories:

type of work	skills required	personality	hours	pay	other benefits

Also, add these words:

full –time   well-paid   friendly part time   patient boring

computer skills   independent   30 days holiday leadership skills

low paid   driving licence overtime   interesting   organised   languages

medical insurance scheme   pensionable to work under pressure

Exercise 2

Find all the adjectives from the words above, e.g. patient, and write the nouns:

Exercise 3

Now think about two different jobs, including your own, if you have one, and write a description for each. When you finish swap your descriptions with your partner and see if there are any similarities between the jobs.

Out There Task

VoIP - Visit http://jobs.guardian.co.uk/ to find jobs.

Real world - visit a job centre.

Find at least four jobs that you find interesting. Find out the details for each job; write about what skills or personality is needed and any other details about the job.

Job Title:	Job Title:
Description: Skills /personality:	Description: Skills /personality:
Job Title:	Job Title:
Description: Skills /personality:	Description: Skills /personality

VoIP

Speak to your conversation partners and find out which of these jobs they would/wouldn't like to do and why. Tell them about which of these jobs you would/wouldn't do. Remember you can record your conversation.

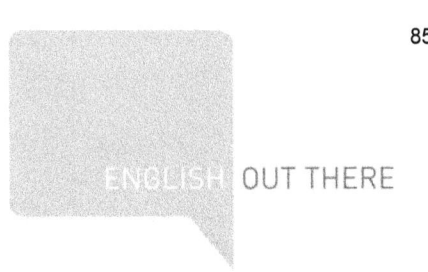

Notes

Lesson Plan

Level 4	Topic	Aim	Language Focus	Skills
Lesson 13	The weather – how does it affect you?	To enable students to talk about the weather and how it makes them feel	Weather vocabulary, expressing emotions, feelings	Speaking, reading, listening

Out There – real world	*Out There* – VoIP
Take the class to a well-populated area of the town or city, somewhere where people are not in a rush and are easy to approach (i.e. sitting down).	Tell students to call conversation partners using VoIP.

#	Details	Task Sheet	Minutes
1	To introduce the aim and task of the day, tell the students how weather affects you – I like sunny weather/I don't like the cold. Then ask them to talk about their weather likes and dislikes with a partner. Give them a few moments to think how it affects them. Listen to their answers and write some on the board, highlighting any errors. Explain the focus of the lesson.		10
2	Give out Task Sheet 1 and ask the students to work through the weather exercises. A: matching weather conditions, B: word order wind and temp, C: vocabulary, D: nouns to adjectives. Check answers to each exercise in open class.	1	20
3	Reading: read the text and answer the comprehension questions (true or false). Then check for unknown vocabulary. Students discuss points in pairs.	2	20
4	Elicit and write vocabulary expressing feelings on the board. Include: happy, relaxed, refreshed, invigorated, excited, energised, full of beans, I don't give a toss, sad, depressed, gloomy, etc.		10
5	Discuss 'how the weather makes you feel'. Use pictures of weather conditions to practise the adjectives of feeling.		10
6	Explain the *Out There* task. Go through the questions and discuss some possible answers.	3	10

	Out There Tasks		
7	**Real world:** Students ask members of the public their questions to start conversations.	**VoIP:** Students ask conversation partners their questions to start conversations.	40
8	**Feedback:** Ask how it went. Check the students have completed the task. Ask them to list their favourite new expressions and words of the day. Ask if they feel confident with the language taught and get feedback.	**Feedback:** Same as real world when in class, but also think about having students do the task as homework, record it and email it to you as an assessment.	45

© 2007/2008 Languages Out There and its licensors. Reproduction in whole or in part prohibited except as may be provided under the terms of a Licence Agreement. www.languagesoutthere.com

Task Sheet 1

Weather conditions

A. Match the meanings with the phrases:

Rain:

a. when it rains for a short period of time, we call it	it's overcast.
b. when it is raining a lot we might say	it's pouring (or it's pouring with rain).
c. If the rain is very light we say	a shower.
d. when the sky is heavy with clouds we say	it's drizzling, or a drizzle.

Snow:

e. when it snows heavily, we call it	sleet
f. when the snow comes down as little balls of ice, we call it	a snowstorm or a blizzard.
g. when the snow is mixed with rain, it's called	hail

B. Wind: put these words in order from the most gentle to something that is more than 100 km per hour:

a gale / a breeze / a hurricane / a strong wind / a wind

_____ _____ _____ _____ _____

Temperature: put these words in order from the lowest temperature to the highest:

Mild / chilly / hot / cold / warm / boiling / freezing

_____ _____ _____ _____ _____ _____ _____

What do you think is a cold temperature? A hot temperature? The perfect temperature?

C. Thunderstorms: A spell (a period of time) of very hot weather often ends with a thunderstorm. First it becomes very humid (hot and wet), then there is thunder (which you hear) and lightning (which you see), and finally, very heavy rain (it pours with rain). Afterwards, it is usually cooler and feels fresher.

D. Describe the weather: find the adjective deriving from the nouns below:

sun	It's _____
cloud	_____
fog	_____
wind	_____
ice	_____
heat	_____
cold	_____
humidity	_____

Task Sheet 2

A visitor talking about British weather:

Everyone knows that when two British people meet in the street or on a train, the first thing they talk about is the weather. They say things like 'Nice day, isn't it?' or 'A bit fresh this morning, isn't it?' In my country no-one talks about the weather because it's always the same. Hot and sunny every day!

I never understood why the British were so obsessed with the weather until I first went to London to study English. I remember one particular day in August last year. I remember the day really well. In fact I remember it as if it was yesterday! I got up early to catch the bus to school. It was a bright, clear summer's morning with a blue sky and a few fluffy clouds. I remember thinking it was a typical English summer's day – the kind you read about in 1950s novels. I wore a t-shirt and shorts and, because it was summer, a pair of open-toed sandals. As I waited at the bus-stop I was sweating in the warm sun.

I got off the bus and started to walk towards the school. It was a 10-minute walk and I had plenty of time so I wasn't hurrying. As I walked along I noticed that the sky had gone dark and was full of black angry-looking clouds. I started to walk a bit faster. A few large drops of rain began to fall. Then s strong wind started blowing. Within seconds it was pouring with rain and I was soaked to the skin. I started running and finally found some shelter in a shop doorway. I stood their shivering in my wet t-shirt. My feet were so cold that they actually turned blue! After five minutes or so it finally stopped raining and I set off to walk the last few hundred metres to the school. Then, as suddenly as they had come, the clouds disappeared. The sun came out again and I arrived at the school in hot sunshine. My clothes were almost dry.

I was at school for about six hours. During this period the sun had shone and it had been hot in the classroom. I had dried out completely and had forgotten about my morning ordeal. I left school at around four o'clock and set off to walk to the bus-stop. It was so hot that sweat was pouring down my face. Then I heard a low noise in the distance. It was thunder. All of a sudden the sky turned black again and the wind got up. I ran for the nearest shop doorway. Suddenly huge hailstones began falling from the sky. Some of them were as big as golf balls. Within minutes the whole street was covered in a white layer. It looked like snow. I was amazed. Four seasons in one day! No wonder the British talk about the weather!

Are these statements true or false?

- The visitor came to London to study English.
- He took the underground to school.
- It was raining when he left home.
- His t-shirt was almost dry when he got to school.
- It was cloudy and cold when he left school.
- He sheltered in a bus-stop.
- He was surprised how changeable the weather was.

Discuss with your partner how you would feel if you were in London on this day. Some people have strong reactions to the weather. What about you? Find out how your partner often feels in these weather conditions:

On a bright, frosty winter morning

On a warm summer's evening just as the sun is setting

On a hot and humid summer's day

On a wet and windy November day

By the sea on a stormy day

Out There Task

Real World - When you first approach people say: "Excuse me, I am learning English. Can I ask you some questions please?"

VoIP - Call conversation partners and ask them these questions to start a conversation. Remember you can record your conversation to listen to later!

Ask these questions and talk about how the weather makes you feel:

Q1. How do you feel on a warm summer's evening just as the sun is setting?

Q2. How do you feel on a wet and windy day in November?

Q3. How do you feel on a bright frosty winter morning?

Q4. How do you feel on a hot, humid summer's day with thunder rumbling in the distance?

Q5. How do you feel when you wake up in the morning to find it has snowed heavily overnight?

Lesson Plan

Level 4	Topic	Aim	Language Focus	Skills
Lesson 14	Fears	To talk about fears and phobias, using past tenses	Past perfect vs past simple	Speaking, reading, listening

Out There – real world	*Out There* – VoIP
Take students to a place where people are hanging out and not in a rush. They are generally more approachable if they are sitting down. Think parks, squares and civic spaces where people take a break from their busy day.	Tell students to call conversation partners on VoIP using the school's computers or at home.

#	Details	Task Sheet	Minutes
1	To introduce the task, write on the board: 'When I arrived at the castle, I remembered that I ___ been there before.' Ask the class to fill the gap (had) and continue the story (write 1-2 lines). Explain the aim of the lesson.		10
2	Reading task (remember to cut up before class): ask the students to work in pairs and put the sections of the article in the correct order.	1	15
3	Give the students the complete version and let them check their answers. Then ask them to answer the comprehension questions and focus on the differences between the tenses used.	2	15
4	Presentation of past perfect. Focus on the form, time line, time expressions used and when the tense is used. Quickly refer to past continuous and past perfect continuous and the differences between them.	3	10
5	Tell the students to do Exercise 1: the past perfect v past simple gap fill. Help with intonation.		10
6	Tell the students to match the phobias and meanings. Check in open class.	4	15
7	Explain the *Out There* task.		5

	Out There Tasks		
8	**Real world:** Students ask members of the public their questions to start conversations.	**VoIP:** Students ask conversation partners their questions to start conversations.	40
9	**Feedback:** Ask how it went. Check the students have completed the task. Ask them to list their favourite new expressions and words of the day. Ask if they feel confident with the language taught and get feedback.	**Feedback:** Same as real world when in class, but also think about having students do the task as homework, record it and email it to you as an assessment.	45

© 2007/2008 Languages Out There and its licensors. Reproduction in whole or in part prohibited except as may be provided under the terms of a Licence Agreement. www.languagesoutthere.com

Task Sheet 1

A Dorset woman found a poisonous black widow spider in a bunch of bananas.
It was the size of a 50 pence piece and had the tell-tale triangular red markings on its abdomen.
She had eaten two of the bananas before spotting the spider but then used a spoon to push it into a plastic container.
A bite can cause a severe reaction and can be fatal in some circumstances.
Vicki Bell, from Weymouth, contacted the police and then the RSPCA who sent an inspector to collect it.
She said: "I went to tell the greengrocer that he should check his bananas more carefully in the future"
"It wasn't very pleasant to think I had been rummaging about in that bag twice not knowing it was there"
The *Daily Mail* reports the spider ended up at Bristol Zoo where expert Warren Spencer identified it. He said: "They are potentially fatal to everyone, from the cradle to the grave, but different people react differently.
"My guess is that it came from Central America – it's certainly not from around here"

Task Sheet 2
Woman finds deadly spider in the bananas

A Dorset woman found a poisonous black widow spider in a bunch of bananas.

It was the size of a 50 pence piece and had the tell-tale triangular red markings on its abdomen.

She had eaten two of the bananas before spotting the spider but then used a spoon to push it into a plastic container.

A bite can cause a severe reaction and can be fatal in some circumstances.

Vicki Bell, from Weymouth, contacted the police and then the RSPCA who sent an inspector to collect it.

She said: "I went to tell the greengrocer that he should check his bananas more carefully in the future"

"It wasn't very pleasant to think I had been rummaging about in that bag twice not knowing it was there"

The *Daily Mail* reports the spider ended up at Bristol Zoo where expert Warren Spencer identified it. He said: "They are potentially fatal to everyone, from the cradle to the grave, but different people react differently.

"My guess is that it came from Central America – it's certainly not from around here".

Comprehension questions:

1. Where was he spider found?
2. What happens to the victim of a black widow bite?
3. What did Vicki Bell do when she spotted it?
4. What did she tell the greengrocer?
5. Where is the spider now?
6. What different verb tenses can you find in the text? Write down examples:

   -
   -
   -

7. Discuss with a partner: When is the past perfect tense used? What information does it give us?
8. What is the difference between these sentences:

   When John arrived home at 8pm Rachel cooked dinner

   When John arrived home at 8pm Rachel had cooked dinner

   When John arrived home at 8pm Rachel was cooking dinner

Task Sheet 3

Past perfect: copy what your teacher writes on the board.

Form:

When

After

****

Exercise 1: Put the verbs in brackets in the past simple or past perfect

1. I (feel) _____ embarrassed that I (make) _____ such a stupid mistake.

2. Nobody (come) _____ to the party because Veronica (forgot) _____ to tell anyone about it.

3. I (know) _____ that I _____ (leave) my keys on the table.

4. Before the police (arrive) _____ the suspect (destroy) _____ all the evidence.

5. He couldn't find the CD that I (lend) _____ him.

6. We (be) _____ pleased we (not invest) _____ our money in that company.

7. They (think) _____ he (leave) _____ earlier.

8. It was a film that I (never heard) _____ of.

9. She (be) _____ not sure, where she (put) _____ her passport.

10. When I (arrive) _____ the film (already start) _____ .

Task Sheet 4

Guess the Phobia

Match the name of the phobia with the meaning:

1	Arithmophobia	A	Bulls
2	Bibliophobia	B	France or the French
3	Melanophobia	C	Animals
4	Logophobia	D	Computers
5	Graphophobia	E	Words
6	Octophobia	F	Anything new
7	Zoophobia	G	Numbers
8	Claustrophobia	H	The colour black
9	Taurophobia	I	The number 8
10	Cyberphobia	J	Books
11	Agoraphobia	K	Outer space
12	Phobophobia	L	Bicycles
13	Neophobia	M	Telephones
14	Spacephobia	N	Englishness
15	Anglophobia	O	Writing
16	Xenophobia	P	Crowded public places
17	Phonophobia	Q	Night
18	Cyclophobia	R	Foreigners or strangers
19	Gallophobia	S	Confined spaces
20	Noctiphobia	T	Phobias

© 2007/2008 Languages Out There and its licensors. Reproduction in whole or in part prohibited except as may be provided under the terms of a Licence Agreement. www.languagesoutthere.com

Out There Task

Real world - say: "Excuse me, I am learning English. Can I ask you some questions please?" then ask people these questions below. Listen to the verbs used in people's stories.

VoIP – Call your conversation partners and ask them these questions to start a conversation. Remember you can record your conversation to listen to later. Listen to the verbs used in people's stories.

Do you have any phobias?

What else are you scared of?

What other phobias do you know the names of?

Do you know any scary stories or situations when you have been afraid? What happened?

Lesson Plan

Level 4	Topic	Aim	Language Focus	Skills
Lesson 15	Music	To review and talk about music	Adjectives to describe music	Reading, writing, listening, speaking

Out There – real world	Out There – VoIP
Find a place close to the school where lots of people are sitting down relaxing, like a small park or a square. Tell students not to forget to use the 'magic words' and to smile! Or visit a music store.	Tell students to call conversation partners on VoIP using the school's computers or at home.

#	Details	Task Sheet	Minutes
1	To introduce the aim and task of the day, ask the students what was the last CD/music download they bought. Ask them to describe the music style and give as much detail as they can. Use the answers to explain the focus and aim of the lesson.		5
2	Elicit a spider diagram of different types of music and give examples of well-known proponents of each. Then ask the students to discuss the questions on music in pairs/groups.	1	15
3	Hand out Task Sheet 2. Ask the students to read the review and answer the comprehension questions. Check the vocabulary and drill for pronunciation.	2	20
4	Students write a paragraph to practise reviewing. Monitor and check reviews.	3	20
5	Tell the students to match the idioms to their meanings. Students choose three idioms and write sentences. Check and help with pronunciation.	3	20
6	Explain the *Out There* task.		5

	Out There Tasks		
7	**Real world:** Students ask members of the public their questions to start conversations. Or they listen to music and read reviews to enable them to write a review.	**VoIP:** Students ask conversation partners their questions to start conversations.	40
8	**Feedback:** Ask how it went. Give students time to write a review. Monitor and check the reviews. Ask the students to list their favourite new expressions and words of the day. Ask if they are happy with what they have learnt today.	**Feedback:** Same as real world when in class, but also think about having students do the task as homework, record it and email it to you as an assessment.	45

Task Sheet 1

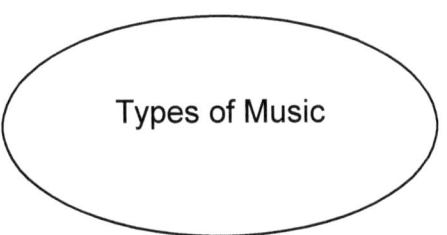

What kind of songs do you listen to:

- at a party
- on a journey
- when you get home in the evening
- first thing in the morning
- when you are studying
- at a concert

Do you think listening to songs helps you learn English? Why?

What songs would you recommend to somebody learning English? Why?

Task Sheet 2

Read my lips.

****

Take this album home with you now! 5th September

Reviewer: A music fan from London

Here is the long-awaited debut album from Sophie Ellis-Bextor, the girl that rather famously and gloriously kept Posh Spice from the number one throne with Spiller last year. Now she's on her own and it isn't half bad. Ellis-Bextor has managed to do something that so few pop stars can nowadays; keep it pop, yet sophisticated and stylish. With the magnificent 'Take me home' and equally good tracks 'Lover', 'Murder on the dance floor' and 'I believe' Ellis-Bextor she can definitely sing and write (all tracks are co-written by her).

A couple of tracks are a bit weaker ('Sparkle', 'Final move') but on the whole it's extremely strong. With an album this good under her belt at the tender age of 22, I can only wonder what gem of an album she'll come up with next.

Look at the review of Sophie Ellis-Bextor's album.

1. Quickly read through and underline five adjectives the reviewer uses to describe her album.

2. Read the review again and put the following information in the correct order as it appears in the review. Number 3 has been done for you.

- good tracks
- album title
- the singer's future
- the singer's background (3)
- music style
- star rating
- bad tracks

3. Is the style formal or informal?

4. Does the reviewer like the album? How do you know?

5. How many times does the reviewer use 'I'? Why?

6. Does it make you want to hear the album? Why/why not?

Task Sheet 3

Think about music you have heard recently. Write a paragraph about it (50-70 words). Swap with your partner and see if you would buy the music they reviewed.

Review

Musical Idioms

Match the idiom to the meaning:

Idiom	Meaning
1. to drum something in	A. to keep saying something until it is remembered
2. to tweak the heartstrings	B. to say you are good at something
3. to blow one's own trumpet	C. to make someone feel sympathetic
4. to drum up business	D. to tell everything
5. to sing like a canary	E. to get interest in a company
6. to sing at the top of one's voice	F. to play the piano
7. to tickle the ivories	G. to sing or make noise to let someone know you are near

Now write three sentences using the idioms above:

*

*

*

Out There Task

Real world – say to people: "Excuse me, I am learning English. Can I ask you some questions please?"

VoIP - Call conversation partners and ask them these questions to start a conversation. Remember you can record your conversation to listen to later.

What was the last CD/music download you bought?

What type of music is it?

What are your favourite bands and types of music?

Why do you like these bands and types of music?

What is your favourite album ever? Can you describe it to me please?

© 2007/2008 Languages Out There and its licensors. Reproduction in whole or in part prohibited except as may be provided under the terms of a Licence Agreement. www.languagesoutthere.com

Out There Task

1. In the music store, look at music magazines and read some reviews. Look at the language used and take notes:

2. Listen to CD's from different genres and take notes on one you like, to use for a review later:

Now write a review of the CD you listened to:

Lesson Plan

Level 4	Topic	Aim	Language Focus	Skills
Lesson 16	Food	To enable students to discuss food and find out people's favourite dishes	Vocabulary on food preparation and phrases	Listening, speaking, reading

Out There – real world	*Out There* – VoIP
Take the class to a well-populated area of the town or city, somewhere where people are not in a rush and are easy to approach (i.e. sitting down).	Tell students to call conversation partners using VoIP.

#	Details	Task Sheet	Minutes
1	To introduce the aim and task of the lesson, ask the class what they think is the most popular dish/cuisine in the UK (answer: Indian). Ask them to describe how most Indian dishes are prepared. Use answers to introduce the focus of the lesson.		5
2	Elicit/explain the different phrases for levels of hunger. Tell the students to match the verb with the most appropriate food item. Check in open class. Ask the students to work in pairs to discuss the ingredients, recipes, ways of cooking etc of traditional dishes. Check in open class.	1	25
3	Tell the students to write the verb next to the correct picture. Elicit any other ways of cooking and preparing food. Also elicit 'raw'.	2	10
4	Recipe reading activity: tell the students to put the recipe in the correct order. Explain any new vocabulary and drill for pronunciation. Key: 3, 8, 6, 1, 9, 7, 5, 2, 4, 10. Collocations: ask the students to do the matching exercise in pairs. Ways of eating: go through the verbs and ask the students to fill the gaps. Check answers in open class.	3	25
5	Then students write a recipe of a dish they like and tell a partner. Monitor and help with pronunciation.		10
6	Explain the *Out There* task.		5

	Out There Tasks		
7	**Real world:** Students ask members of the public about preparing their favourite meals.	**VoIP:** Students ask conversation partners about preparing their favourite meals.	40
8	**Feedback:** Ask how it went. Check the students have completed the task. Check for any new vocabulary. Ask the students to list their favourite new expressions and words of the day. Ask if they feel confident with the language taught and get feedback. Ask if they are hungry now.	**Feedback:** Same as real world when in class, but also think about having students do the task as homework, record it and email it to you as an assessment.	45

© 2007/2008 Languages Out There and its licensors. Reproduction in whole or in part prohibited except as may be provided under the terms of a Licence Agreement. www.languagesoutthere.com

Task Sheet 1

Food

1. Are you hungry? (Pick an answer)

   I'm full / I'm a bit peckish / I'm starving / I'm famished / My stomach is rumbling / I'm all right, cheers

Food preparation

2. Match the verb with the food item it is most often associated with:

   1. to crack — an orange
   2. to grate — a pancake
   3. to knead — a nut
   4. to peel — a rabbit
   5. to skin — a joint of meat
   6. to slice — dough
   7. to carve — a loaf
   8. to mince — cream
   9. to shell — meat
   10. to toss — a hard-boiled egg
   11. to whip — eggs
   12. to stuff — a cake
   13. to mash — a chicken
   14. to beat — cheese
   15. to ice — potatoes

3. Do you know what you should do to prepare the dishes below?

Dish	Main ingredients	Preparation
fish and chips		
full English breakfast		
Sunday lunch		
bangers and mash		
shepherd's pie		
steak and kidney pudding		
spotted dick		

© 2007/2008 Languages Out There and its licensors. Reproduction in whole or in part prohibited except as may be provided under the terms of a Licence Agreement. www.languagesoutthere.com

Task Sheet 2

Match the words and pictures

frying   deep frying   roasting   toasting   stewing

BBQ-ing   baking   steaming

a   b   c   d

e   f   g   h

Write down any words or phrases related to the pictures above. Add any other ways of cooking:

Task Sheet 3

Recipe

Here is a traditional English recipe but it is not in the correct order. Can you put it in the correct order?

Shepherd's Pie

1. Add the minced beef to the onions, stir and fry gently until the meat is brown.
2. Cover the mixture with a layer of mashed potato and bake in the oven for 20 minutes until the potato is golden brown.
3. Begin by boiling the potatoes for 20 minutes until they are soft.
4. Serve with peas, beans, cauliflower or other fresh vegetables.
5. Add a little butter and milk to the potatoes and mash them thoroughly.
6. Chop the onions and fry in vegetable oil in a frying pan until light brown.
7. Pour the mixture into a baking dish.
8. Place the mashed potato to one side until later.
9. Then add the beef stock to the pan, bring to the boil and simmer for 10 minutes.
10. Eat.

Match a and b below, e.g. black coffee:

stale	rotten	roasted	black	rich	fattening	bruised	bland	healthy
dessert	bread	apple	foods	potatoes	sauce	diet	coffee	eggs

Ways of eating

Put each of the following verbs into its correct place in the sentence:

chew lick polish off swallow gnaw consume peck at gorge digest bolt

1. The children have no appetite. They just _____ their food. They hardly eat anything.
2. My mother always used to say to me 'Now make sure you _____ meat carefully before you _____ it.'
3. Statistics show that we _____ more fruit and meat than 10 years ago.
4. He has an enormous appetite. I've just seen him _____ four hamburgers and a pile of chips.
5. As children we used to _____ ourselves on ice-cream, chips and chocolate and then feel very sick.
6. The starving prisoners were so desperate they would _____ any meat bones they could find.
7. It's not good for your body to ____ your food so quickly. Eat slowly so that you can _____ it properly.
8. He was so hungry that when he'd finished his food, he began to ____ the plate!

Your recipe:

Out There Task

Ask people about their favourite dishes and how they are prepared. Get as many details as possible: ingredients, preparation, serving. Then tell them about your favourite meal.

Real world - say: "Excuse me, I am learning English. Can I ask you some questions please?"

VoIP - Call conversation partners and ask them about their favourite dishes. Remember you can record your conversation to listen to later.

What is your favourite meal and how exactly do you prepare it?

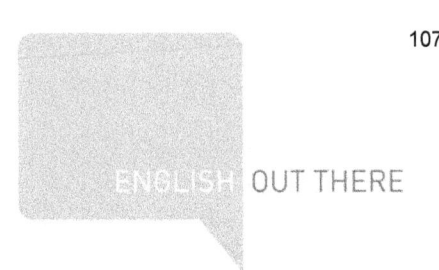

Notes

Lesson Plan

Level 4	Topic	Aim	Language Focus	Skills
Lesson 17	Lottery	To talk about what you would do if you were a millionaire	Second conditional	Reading, speaking listening

Out There – real world	*Out There* – VoIP
In a department store or large shop.	Tell students to call conversation partners using VoIP.

#	Details	Task Sheet	Minutes
1	To introduce the aim and task of the day, ask students what they would do if they won £1 million. 'What do you think about the lottery? Do you play it? Do you know anyone or have you heard about anyone who has?' On the board, write 'If I ___ the lottery…' Ask the class to complete the sentence. Use answers/mistakes to explain the aim of the lesson.		10
2	Reading: lottery millionaires. Ask the students to read the text and put the phrases in the gaps. Check vocabulary. Ask: 'How do you think you would change? Would it be a good or bad thing to win so much money?'	1	30
3	Second conditional: elicit the form and the use (to imagine a different present or future unreal/unlikely situation) and write them on the board for students to copy. Tell the students to write some examples. Point out the use of 'were' in expressions like 'if I were you…' Then ask them to complete the sentences and compare answers.	2	15
4	Students complete second conditional sentences with correct verb form as in the example given. Check answers in the group, monitor and help with pronunciation if necessary. Students write five sentences using second conditional. Monitor and then check in open class.	3	15
5	Explain the *Out There* task. Point out the rules to the task, not going over £50k and only one item per department.		10

	Out There Tasks		
6	**Real world:** Competition: students plan what they would buy up to, but not over £50,000.	**VoIP:** Competition: students plan what they would buy up to, but not over £50,000. Then tell their conversation partners and ask questions.	40
7	**Feedback:** Ask how it went. Check the students have completed the task. See who won! Ask the students to list their favourite new expressions and words of the day. Ask if they feel confident with the language taught and get feedback.	**Feedback:** Same as real world when in class, but also think about having students do the task as homework, record it and email it to you as an assessment.	45

© 2007/2008 Languages Out There and its licensors. Reproduction in whole or in part prohibited except as may be provided under the terms of a Licence Agreement. www.languagesoutthere.com

Task Sheet 1

Lottery millionaires

Read the article. The following words and phrases have been taken out of the text. Where do you think they should go?

- put your feet up
- splashed out
- 'nothing but misery'
- small beer
- mind-blowing
- extravagant

El Gordo, which literally means 'the fat one' is the national lottery of Spain. The main draw is made just before Christmas each year. The prizes are amounts of money that are almost unimaginable. Last year, for example, the total prize money was £ 1,500,000,000. Sometimes the winning prize is shared by an entire community. In December 1999, for example, the inhabitants of the southern Spanish town of Elche shared an incredible £160 million.

This, however, is (1) _____ compared to the prizes that can be won playing Powerball, the largest lottery game in the United States. In December 2002, Andrew Whittaker of West Virginia won a (2) _____ £190 million. When tax and other charges were deducted he ended up with a cool £100 million. Not a bad return on a $10 ticket!

Have you ever wondered, however, what it would be like to wake up one morning and find you had won a major prize on the lottery? What if you won £8 million, for example? What would you do with the money? Would you do what a man in Hastings, East Sussex did and buy a football club? Or would you simply put it in the bank, (3) _____ and live off the interest?

Everyone dreams about winning the lottery but, as many people have found, actually winning it can create more problems than it solves. Take Anne Taylor, for example. She won over £3 million and immediately gave up her job as a cook. "I (4) _____. I bought a new house, lots of new clothes, a couple of cars and went on a cruise", she says. "But in the end I just got bored. I actually missed going to work every day and I missed the company of my friends and colleagues."

Peter Boston experienced a different problem when he won over £5 million on the lottery. "At first it was great", he says. "I didn't do anything (5) _____. I didn't move house or buy a luxury car. I didn't give up my job. I just took a couple of weeks' holiday and treated my family to a few presents. The problem was that everybody knew I had won a lot of money on the lottery. After a while people started asking me for money. They wanted me to invest money in all sorts of crazy projects. It got to the stage when I didn't know who my friends were any more. I didn't know if they were real friends or if they simply wanted to know me because I was a millionaire. I don't think I'll be happy again until the money's all gone. In the end I can honestly say the lottery brought me (6) _____."

Task Sheet 2

Second conditional

Form:
+   +

Use:

Example:

Finish these sentences in your own words:

1. If I saw a ghost I ...

2. If I had my life all over again I ...

3. If I had two days to live I ...

4. If I could live anywhere in the world I ...

5. If I found £10,000 in the street I ...

6. If I had to change my job I ...

7. If I were president of my country I ...

8. If I could be someone else I ...

9. If I could meet a famous person I ...

10. If I were an animal I ...

Task Sheet 3

Put the correct verb form in the sentences that describe imaginary situations. Then complete the sentences in a suitable way.

Example: Even if the train __was__ (be) late, it __wouldn't matter__ (matter) because __ we haven't got to go to work today.

1. If I _____(lose) my house keys, it _____(not matter).

because_____.

2. If someone _____(steal) my car, I _____ (not be) too concerned.

because_____.

3. If I_____(not pass) my exams this time, it _____(not be) too bad.

because_____.

4. It_____(not matter) if I _____(forget) to do my homework today.

because_____.

5. It _____ (be) terrible if I_____(lose) my passport.

because_____.

6. If I_____ (lose) my driving licence, it _____(be) terrible.

because_____.

Write five sentences using the second conditional:

-

-

-

-

-

Out There Task

Real world – In a department store.

VoIP – Visit an online department website like www.johnlewis.com.

If I had £50,000 I would buy…

In the department store you have to choose things you **would buy** if you **had** to spend £50,000.

Rules:
- you can only buy one item from each department
- minimum five items
- write down a description of what you would buy why you would buy it and how much it costs
- you cannot spend more that £50,000. The closest to £50,000 is the winner, not one penny over!

VoIP: now tell your conversation partners what you would buy for £50,000. Ask these questions to start a conversation:

What would you do if you won the lottery?

What do you think about the lottery and how it affects people who win?

Notes

Lesson Plan

Level 4	Topic	Aim	Language Focus	Skills
Lesson 18	Queues	To discuss the issue of queuing, helpful or annoying	Vocabulary on cultural differences	Reading, speaking, listening

Out There – real world	Out There – VoIP
Find a place close to the school where lots of people are sitting down relaxing, like a small park or a square. Tell students not to forget to use the 'magic words' and to smile!	Tell students to call conversation partners on VoIP client using the school's computers or at home.

#	Details	Task Sheet	Minutes
1	To introduce the aim and task of the day, make the students stand up and form a line, standing one behind the other. Ask them what they are doing. Elicit the word queue. Ask what was the last thing they queued for.		5
2	Give out Task Sheet 1 and ask the students to discuss the questions in pairs. Listen to their ideas in the group.	1	15
3	Hand out Task Sheet 2. Ask the students to read the short extract.	2	10
4	Ask the students to work with a partner and write down what they can remember without looking at the text; check what each pair has remembered.	2	15
5	Ask the students to read the text again; check for new vocabulary.	2	10
6	Task Sheet 3: in pairs or small groups students discuss what they would say in the situations. Elicit possible responses and write a few possibilities for each on the board.	3	20
7	Give details of the *Out There* task.		5

Out There Tasks			
8	**Real world:** Students ask members of the public their questions to start conversations.	**VoIP:** Students ask conversation partners their questions to start conversations.	40
9	**Feedback:** Ask how it went. Check the students have completed the task. Ask them to list their favourite new expressions and words of the day. Ask if they feel confident with the language taught and get feedback.	**Feedback:** Same as real world when in class, but also think about having students do the task as homework, record it and email it to you as an assessment.	45

© 2007/2008 Languages Out There and its licensors. Reproduction in whole or in part prohibited except as may be provided under the terms of a Licence Agreement. www.languagesoutthere.com

Task Sheet 1

Do you queue?

Discuss your answers to these questions with a partner:

1. Do people queue in your country?

2. Are you a patient person or an impatient person?

3. What is the maximum amount of time you would queue?
   - to buy a ticket for a concert where your favourite band is playing
   - to buy a ticket for a cup final when you favourite team is playing
   - to see a doctor or a dentist
   - to collect a free gift
   - to check in at an airport
   - to buy the latest computer game

4. Do you queue for things in other countries that you would not queue for at home?

5. Have you ever seen people getting angry in a queue?

Task Sheet 2

To queue or not to queue?

Read what these people say about queuing:

A. "I hate queuing. I can honestly say that it's one of the few activities that I really can't stand. I hate waiting to buy a train ticket, for example. Your train is leaving in five minutes and there's always some idiot in front of you who wants to renew his season ticket or ask the time of the last train to Glasgow on July 23rd next year. I want to kill people like that."

B. "I think queuing is one of the hallmarks of a civilised society. Queuing is polite. It shows consideration for your fellow human beings. People who stand in a queue in a patient, orderly manner also demonstrate that they have an understanding of fair play and the idea of 'first come, first served'. If everyone follows the rules, queuing is perfectly acceptable."

C. "I think the British, in particular, are obsessed with queuing. They queue in banks, at the post-office, in shops, at bus-stops, waiting for taxis. I think they actually enjoy it in a strange sort of way. The funniest thing is to watch British people in the departure lounge at airports, especially abroad. They start queuing at the gate even before the flight has been called. I can't imagine why. Do they think the flight is going to leave without them?"

D. "I think queuing is OK as long as everybody follows the rules. If you're waiting in a queue at a taxi rank and then someone pushes in at the front of the queue, that's really annoying. The problem is that most British people are too polite to say anything. They just shrug their shoulders and ignore it. Imagine if everyone pushed in at the front. What would happen then?"

E. "I queued for tickets for the Centre Court at Wimbledon. We turned up at eight o'clock the previous evening. We took sleeping bags, hot drinks and sandwiches. I had my iPod too, and a book to read. We thought we would be first in the queue and get the best seats. Just imagine how we felt when we got there and found there were several hundred people in front of us! We queued until for over 13 hours but we got our tickets. I think it was worth it in the end."

F. "I was at the front of the queue for the New Year's day sale at a big department store in Oxford Street. They were selling a £2,000 coat for £10 and I was determined to have it. I started queuing at 3pm the previous day and when they opened the doors at 9am the next morning, I was first through the door. I ran up the escalator and got there first. That was the only time I've ever wanted to queue!"

What examples of queuing can you remember from these short extracts? Talk to a partner and write down as many as you can:

-
-
-
-
-

Task Sheet 3

Talk to your partner again. What would you say or do in these situations in queues:

1. You have been waiting for over an hour in a queue for a taxi. You are almost at the front of the queue when two people push in at the front. What would you say?

2. You are waiting to check in at an airport in a very long queue. The two people in front of you are chatting excitedly to each other and you can see that the queue has already moved on by at least 20 metres. What would you do or say?

3. You are in a queue waiting to buy a ticket for a popular rock concert. You need to go to the loo over the road but you don't want to lose you place in the queue. What would you say to the person behind you?

4. Some people are queuing to buy bread in a baker's shop but you are not sure where the end of the queue is. What do you say?

5. You are waiting to check in at an airport in a very long queue. Your flight leaves in 20 minutes. You notice that the people in front of you have a flight leaving in three hours' time. What would you say?

Out There Task

Real world - say: 'Excuse me, I am learning English. Can I ask you some questions please?'

Ask people the following questions. Try to get as much information and detail from them as possible about queuing. You should talk to at least five people.

VoIP – Call conversation partners and ask them these questions to start a conversation. Remember you can record your conversation to listen to later.

1. How many times a day do you queue for things?

2. What do you have to queue for?

3. How patient are you when you queue?

4. How long would you be prepared to queue for the following?

    - to use a public phone box

    - to get tickets for your favourite band / signer

    - to get a visa for a country you want to visit

    - to see a doctor about back pain

    - to get money form a cash machine

    - to get on a bus or tube

5. Do you think it is OK to push in a queue? In what circumstances?

6. Have you ever been abroad and had to queue for something that you would not queue for at home? What?

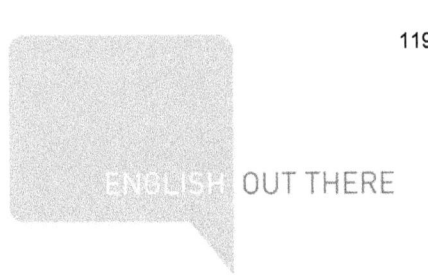

Notes

Lesson Plan

Level 4	Topic	Aim	Language Focus	Skills
Lesson 19	Health problems, treatments and advice	To enable students to discuss health and find treatments	Vocabulary related to common health problems, remedies and advice	Reading, listening, speaking

Out There – real world	*Out There* – VoIP
Take students to a place where people are hanging out and not in a rush. They are generally more approachable if they are sitting down. Think parks, squares and civic spaces where people take a break from their busy day.	Tell students to call conversation partners on VoIP using the school's computers or at home.

#	Details	Task Sheet	Minutes
1	To introduce the aim and task of the lesson write the words **aches** and **remedies** on the board and ask the students to give the meaning of these words or synonyms for them.		10
2	Hand out Task Sheet 1: 'I feel awful - in the pharmacy'. Read and work on new vocabulary. Make a list of treatments and remedies on the board (e.g. tablets, syrup, ice pack, plaster/band-aid, bed rest and fluids, etc) and another for related verbs (e.g. to feel better/well, to relieve (pain), to be in good health, to soothe, etc).	1	20
3	Hand out Task Sheet 2. Ask the students to work in pairs and do the exercises on injuries (prepositions gap fill, match the phrases with meanings and problems with advice).	2	20
4	Discuss similar cases or other conditions the students might have had and give advice or suggest remedies they know. Encourage students to use new vocabulary and revise vocabulary for giving advice.		15
5	Task Sheet 3: ask the students to do the phrasal verb matching exercise. Give examples of each verb in a context (e.g. I need to lose weight so I'm going to take up jogging).	3	10
6	Explain the *Out There* task.		5

	Out There Tasks		
7	**Real world:** Students ask members of the public their advice for remedies and treatments.	**VoIP:** Students ask conversation partners their advice for remedies and treatments.	40
8	**Feedback:** Ask how it went. Check the students have completed the task. Compare remedies. Ask the students to list their favourite new expressions and words of the day. Ask if they feel confident with the language taught and get feedback.	**Feedback:** Same as real world when in class, but also think about having students do the task as homework, record it and email it to you as an assessment.	45

© 2007/2008 Languages Out There and its licensors. Reproduction in whole or in part prohibited except as may be provided under the terms of a Licence Agreement. www.languagesoutthere.com

Task Sheet 1

I feel awful - in the pharmacy

Read the text below and underline all the expressions you don't know:

The pharmacy is full of medicines: syrups, tablets (or pills), ointments, plasters, bandages and wound dressings. I haven't been to my GP, so I don't have a prescription. I don't know what to get for my condition. I'd better describe the symptoms to the pharmacist:

Me: 'Hello, I wonder if you can help me. I'm feeling really unwell. I've been sneezing and coughing all day and my head hurts – I must be coming down with something. Can you suggest anything?'

The pharmacist: 'Sure, there are a variety of medicines here in this aisle. This syrup is often recommended by doctors. Do you suffer from any allergies?'

Me: 'Oh yes, I do, I'm allergic to penicillin. Have you got anything without penicillin?'

The pharmacist: 'Let's have a look. There you go. This one should help. Take one tablespoon three times a day after meals. If the symptoms persist for more than three days, you must go and see your GP'.

Me: 'Thank you very much. How much…'

Task Sheet 2

Injuries – work on the language before they happen!

A. Put the correct word from the following list in each space below:

for   on   in   with   to

1. I saw the doctor ____ her surgery.
2. She listened ____ my problems.
3. They treated me ____ a heart problem.
4. I took the prescription ____ the chemist.
5. I had to go ____ hospital for an operation.
6. Something's wrong ____ my back, doctor.
7. They operated ____ him immediately.

B. Match the sentences on the left with their correct meanings on the right:

1) She got a hearing aid
2) She had no appetite
3) She was a bit deaf
4) She was short-sighted

5) She went on a diet
6) She had a headache
7) She cut down on cigarettes

8) She took it easy

a) She couldn't see things far away
b) Her head hurt
c) She didn't want to eat anything
d) She bought something to help her hear better
e) She rested
f) She couldn't hear very clearly
g) She decided to eat and drink only certain things
h) She smoked less

C. For each problem on the left, choose one (or more) piece of advice on the right:

1) I've cut my finger badly
2) I think I've broken my leg
3) I'm always tired
4) I'm smoking too much
5) I've got the flu
6) I'm getting a bit short-sighted

7) I'm going deaf
8) I'm getting fat
9) There's something wrong with my heart
10) I'm drinking too much
11) I've lost my appetite
12) I've got a headache
13) I'm sleeping badl.

a) Go and see a doctor.
b) Take a day or two off work
c) You'll probably need an X-ray
d) Why don't you have your eyes tested?
e) You should go on a diet
f) The chemist will be able to give you something for it
g) Well, you'd better cut down
h) You might need a hearing aid
i) Just take it easy for a few day
j) Go to bed for a few days
k) You should see a specialist
l) You need more exercise
m) You may need an operation

Task Sheet 3

Match the verbs in A to the meanings in B:

	A		B
1	to put on weight	a	to stop using something (e.g. a particular food)
2	to come down with something	b	to recover from an illness, a shock or some bad news
3	to get over something	c	to develop the symptoms of an illness or disease
4	to cut something out completely	d	to start doing an activity (e.g. jogging)
5	to pass out	e	to recover consciousness
6	to cut down (on) something	f	to get heavier
7	to take up	g	to reduce something; to consume less of something
8	to come round	h	to faint or to lose consciousness for a short time.

Out There Task

Real world - say to people: 'Excuse me, I am learning English. Can I ask you some questions please?'

VoIP - Call your conversation partners and ask these questions to start a conversation. Then tell your conversation partners about your remedies and treatments. Remember you can record your conversation.

Ask at least five different people. Get as much information as you can.

"What remedy or treatment do you recommend for… "

Ailment	Remedy or treatment.
a cold	
a cough	
a cut	
a stomach ache	
a headache	
a broken bone	
a bruise	
a toothache	
a sunburn	
a fever/ temperature	

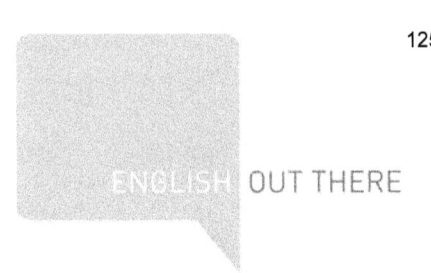

Notes

Lesson Plan

Level 4	Topic	Aim	Language Focus	Skills
Lesson 20	Sleep and dreams	To enable students to find out about dreams and sleep	Connectors and vocabulary related to dreams	Reading, listening, speaking

Out There – real world	*Out There* – VoIP
Find a place close to the school where lots of people are sitting down relaxing, like a small park or a square. Tell students not to forget to use the 'magic words' and to smile!	Tell students to use VoIP to call some conversation partners.

#	Details	Task Sheet	Minutes
1	To introduce the aim and task of the lesson tell the class: 'I slept well, however, I had a bad dream and woke up'. Ask students: 'How did you sleep last night? Did anyone have a dream?' Write the answers on the board and use them to explain the aim.		5
2	Sleep and dreams questions. In pairs students discuss the questions. Check answers in open class. Write new vocabulary on the board and drill pronunciation.	1	15
3	Sleep quiz. Ask the students to work in pairs and discuss the answers to the quiz. Discuss the answers in groups and check any vocabulary. Monitor and help with pronunciation.	2	15
4	Give out Task Sheet 3. Ask the students to read the answers to the quiz and see if they were right. Discuss the answers in open class.	3	15
5	Then ask the students to replace the connectors highlighted in bold with one of the choices in each case.	3	10
6	Elicit these words and phrases: 'connectors used to contrast two pieces of information in a single sentence with the second piece of information being surprising.' Ask the students to write example sentences using three connectors.	3	15
7	Explain the *Out There* task.		5

Out There Tasks		
8	**Real world:** Students ask members of the public their questions to start conversations.	**VoIP:** Students ask conversation partners their questions to start conversations.	40
9	**Feedback:** Ask how it went. Check the students have completed the task. Ask them to list their favourite new expressions and words of the day. Ask if they feel confident with the language taught and get feedback.	**Feedback:** Same as real world when in class, but also think about having Ss do the task as homework, record it and email it to you as an assessment.	45

© 2007/2008 Languages Out There and its licensors. Reproduction in whole or in part prohibited except as may be provided under the terms of a Licence Agreement. www.languagesoutthere.com

Task Sheet 1

Sleep and dreams

How many hours do you usually sleep each night?

Do you think you sleep too much or not enough?

Do you have trouble getting to sleep?

Do you ever wake up in the middle of the night and find that you cannot get back to sleep?

Do you ever sleep during the daytime?

Do you dream?

Do you have a recurring dream (one that happens again and again)?

Do you ever have nightmares?

Can you describe a dream or nightmare you have had?

Do you think it is possible to interpret what dreams mean?

Task Sheet 2

Dream quiz

We spend about 30 per cent of our lives in bed, but how much do we really know about sleep and dreams? Try this quiz with a partner:

1. If you can't sleep, it's best to:

a. try not to think about anything
b. get up for a while
c. count sheep

2. What is the most likely cause of nightmares?

a. stress
b. spicy foods
c. stuffy rooms

3. If you have a problem getting to sleep at night you should:

a. have a couple of glasses of wine before you go to bed
b. go for a long walk just before you go to bed
c. avoid coffee in the evening

4. If you feel tired during the day you should:

a. sleep more at night
b. sleep less at night
c. have regular sleep patterns

5. If you want to sleep well you should:

a. do some energetic exercise during the day
b. sleep in a relaxing environment
c. eat a large meal before bedtime

6. How many hours should you sleep each night?

a. less than 6
b. 6 to 8
c. it depends

7. When do researchers believe we dream the most?

a. when we first go to sleep
b. during deep sleep
c. during REM (rapid eye movement) sleep

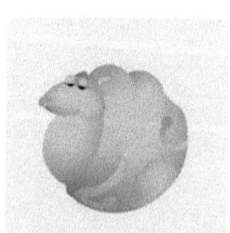

8. Animals dream

a. probably true
b. probably false

Task Sheet 3

A. Answers to quiz. Read the answers to see if you were right:

1 b. If you can't sleep, it's probably better to get up and do something relaxing such as reading a book until you feel tired. **However**, some people may find it useful to count sheep or recite the alphabet in their minds until they fall asleep.

2 a. **Although** no-one is absolutely sure what causes nightmares, most researchers agree that stress is the most likely cause.

3 c. Don't drink any drinks containing significant amounts of caffeine after 2 o'clock in the afternoon. Caffeine and other stimulants can seriously disrupt sleep patterns. A glass of wine shouldn't create sleeping problems but avoid drinking to excess as this can cause dehydration and disrupt sleep significantly.

4 c. Sleeping less certainly won't help and it probably won't make much difference if you start sleeping for a longer period each night. The most important thing is to have a regular routine, going to bed at the same time and getting up at the same time.

5 b. Research has shown that we sleep best in a comfortable and relaxed environment. Bedrooms should not be too hot or cold and there should not be distractions such as noise or light.

6 c. There is no one answer to this question as it depends entirely on the individual. **However**, the vast majority of people seem to find around 7 - 8 hours sleep to be sufficient, **although** some people can get by on less then 5.

7 c. REM is the period during sleep when the brain is most active and this is the time when people dream the most.

8 a. The fact is that we simply don't know. After all, animals can't tell us, can they? **Nevertheless**, many animals do experience REM and there is strong evidence to link REM with dreams – in animals as well as in humans.

B. Can you replace the connecting words in bold in the text above with any of the words below?

- nevertheless/although
- in spite of/even though
- nevertheless/while; despite the fact that/despite
- however/though

C. What do we use these connectors for?

        although, even though, though, despite the fact that, in spite of the fact that.

*
*
*
*

Example:

*
*
*
*
*

Out There Task

Real World - to start your conversations say to people: 'Excuse me, I'm learning English. Can I ask you a few questions please?'

VoIP - Call your conversation partners and ask them these questions to start conversations, tell them about your dreams. Remember you can record your conversations and listen to them later,

Ask people about sleeping and their dreams. Take notes of the answers:

	1	2	3	4	5
Why do people generally remember dreams?					
Please tell me what happened in the last dream you can remember.					
Do you have a recurring dream? What is it about? Why do we have them?					
What happened in the worst nightmare you can remember?					
Have any of your dreams ever come true?					
What do you think you can learn about yourself from your dreams?					
Do you know anything about interpreting dreams?					

© 2007/2008 Languages Out There and its licensors. Reproduction in whole or in part prohibited except as may be provided under the terms of a Licence Agreement. www.languagesoutthere.com

Notes